SUPERYACHT CAPTAIN

SUPERYACHT CAPTAIN

Life and leadership in the world's most incredible industry

Brendan O'Shannassy

ADLARD COLES

LONDON · OXFORD · NEW YORK · NEW DELHI · SYDNEY

ADLARD COLES
Bloomsbury Publishing Plc
50 Bedford Square, London, WC1B 3DP, UK
29 Earlsfort Terrace, Dublin 2, Ireland

BLOOMSBURY, ADLARD COLES and the Adlard Coles logo are
trademarks of Bloomsbury Publishing Plc

First published in 2022

A catalogue record for this book is available from the British Library

Library of Congress Cataloguing-in-Publication data has been
applied for

ISBN: PB: 978-1-4729-9266-6; ePub: 978-1-4729-9264-2;
ePDF: 978-1-4729-9265-9

2 4 6 8 10 9 7 5 3 1

Typeset by Deanta Global Publishing Services, Chennai, India
Printed and bound in Great Britain by CPI Group (UK) Ltd, Croydon
CR0 4YY

To find out more about our authors and books visit
www.bloomsbury.com and sign up for our newsletters

Cover

The cover reflects the power and beauty of a motor yacht as captured by the incredible photo-artist Guillaume Plisson. Guillaume and his team use their lenses to capture yachts in movement and see angles and tones that even the designers were not aware of. Having conducted photo shoots with Guillaume, I am in awe of an artist pushing everyone to find a higher professional plain.

Dedication and Acknowledgments

This book is dedicated to anyone that has ever said to a child, 'you can do it'. A parent, a teacher, a friend, it does not matter; in my story it was a melange of friends' parents and teachers and I thank them all. Their confidence in me when I had none has made all the difference.

It is a well-trodden path for a writer to thank their family and for good reason; my wife Yvonne and daughters Fabienne and Scarlett gave me the purpose to write and more than that they gave me the motivation to follow the career I have. To Yvonne, you are my greatest supporter when most of the time I do not deserve it. To Fabienne and Scarlett, my talented daughters, I am in awe of you both as you explore your worlds and find your own boundaries.

To my parents Allen and Annette. I am sorry our time together was shortened. We shared a stage but only for the first act. Despite knowing you cannot see these words, I still thank you for helping me to find the values I use through life.

Within the yachting community I know that acknowledging all is pithy and excluding any is fraught with risk. Acknowledging the latter, I wish to thank two groups: the yacht owners and the yacht crew.

To the yacht owners, thank you for committing to the adventure of yacht ownership. I have learnt so much from you and have never lost the overwhelming sense of privilege I felt on the first day stepping on a yacht (just before cleaning it).

To the yacht crew, I know how hard you work, how much you seek to deliver a never-ending expression of excellence and how much you misbehave when opportunity allows. For all the good, the bad and the downright unbelievable, I stand alongside you and thank you all.

CONTENTS

PROLOGUE

What could a superyacht captain teach me?

This is a captain's story, my story, where I look back on the physical, emotional and professional challenges that I have faced working in support of the most exclusive client group in the world and their relentless demands. It also charts a journey into the 'heart of brightness' that is the superyacht environment. It took me 15 years to earn the title of Captain and I walk through the narrow lanes, the dead ends and the bumpy distractions to that place.

The world of superyachts is far removed from most of the planet's 'normal'. It is a world where boundaries blur and the everyday rules of life seem to disappear. A world where lessons and insights are not read about and studied, but lived in an environment of constant pressure, where the consequences of actions result in immediate success or failure. This high stakes, no-safety-net workplace provided me with rolling insights that transfer directly for anyone looking for that edge to be their best version of themselves. My lessons are not hypothetical, gathered from postgraduate studies and delivered in a TED talk; I lived through the glory (but mostly the pain) of the constant scrutiny and expectations of billionaire superyacht owners.

A superyacht is also a study in globalisation. Yacht captains do not speak of diversity as a slogan or a company goal: we live it. The crews are multinational and multilingual and disperse around the globe when not on board. The same is true of the owners. It is common for a conversation to cross multiple languages and for all parties to be speaking in their second or third languages. Many businesses operate globally – this is nothing unique – but not many businesses move their office every few weeks to a new country, a different language, a new climate, a different legal system, and are expected to be experts on arrival. This is the expectation placed on a yacht and its captain. Whether it be Monaco, Miami, Palau or Papeete, there is an assumption that the captain will have the intimacy of a local by the time their feet are on the dock. They may have ducked an Atlantic hurricane (or two) during the office relocation, but this is not even considered. The business must be open on arrival. Yes, there are leadership lessons for all from this environment.

A better Bond villain

I will describe my actions in support of and in response to the billionaires I have served. I will peer deeply into their behaviours from my privileged position sitting in their inner sanctums: an area that normally is so fantastic it cannot even be represented in film. Superyachts have completely ruined the Bond franchise for me; when I watch a Bond film – and I love Bond films – I am always disappointed in how under-equipped the villains are, with minimal staff, small yachts and a general lack of resources.

The term 'typical day' does not reflect yacht captaincy. One request from a guest takes the day in a new direction or even to a new location. To the eternal chagrin of my crews, I thrive on this disruption. I see each change as a chance to climb out on my performance edge, a way of freshly testing my creativity and problem-solving capabilities, a chance to see if my leadership can deliver what the team needs when their preferred initial solution has been cast aside on the whim of a guest. Alongside the crew, I bet heavily to deliver an experience that is comparable to the incredible investment of the yacht owner. I draw deep on previous yachts, previous performance and my crew; sometimes I win big and sometimes I fail, the outcome being more dependent on the mood of the client than the efforts of those of us working passionately in the shadows. This is harrowing, but an attraction at the same time.

On one of these 'just another day as a superyacht captain' occasions, I was hosting one of the great modern Hollywood directors for a tour of the yacht. A director so fabled himself that I am sure a movie of his own life will be released if the Marvel back catalogue is ever cleared. I was struck by the inquisitiveness of this world-leading professional; it was intoxicating that he hung off my every word and then probed further with his questions. I found that I was drawing deeper into my knowledge to keep up and wanted to share the glory of this yacht with someone who was clearly interested. With all his success, the director had remained humble, engaged and good-humoured.

As enjoyable as his company was, it was a busy evening and I had hoped to slip through this private tour ahead of the main guests' arrival. There was an intimate pre-party, and the very special of the special guests were already boarding. I was trying not to seem rushed, but my internal anxiety clock was ticking. Conducting the private tour did not allow me to maintain the necessary oversight of the full yacht during the critical guest arrival period.

The tour slowed further as, in addition to the questions the director was asking, we were being greeted by his friends: a tech founder, a global sportsman, an NFL team owner; they shared an intimacy that the yacht afforded. Without anyone having to say anything, they all knew: this was the rarest of air and they were truly the chosen few to inhale it.

Even as the chosen few, they were also aware that they were now in a league that exceeded their own excess by so many multiples that they fell in step with their shared awe. A yacht of this scale is beyond anything an A-list actor, sportsperson or model could imagine. Their not-insignificant net worth would not even pay for the artwork. Indeed, there was one piece on board that I liked, but drew little attention from visitors: at US$80 million, it alone was a lifetime's wealth many times over.

As the director was asking for specifics of the submarine, two other guests who I did not recognise joined us. 'How well can you see out of the curved, thickened acrylic windows?' 'What is the definition of the external cameras?' I was just keeping up with detailed responses when a Formula 1 race driver joined our small group, adding his own questions. 'What control systems are in use and what is the automation allowing the pilot to manoeuvre the bulky craft?' As if scripted, Gio, the charismatic Italian submarine pilot, approached, smiled to my now four tour guests, and asked if I needed help. He picked up the script seamlessly, answering with technical competence as my radio crackled: 'Could the captain come to the helicopter deck?'

I excused myself. The helicopter deck was not a long walk, but my pace was slowed by guests who sought to greet 'The Captain'. I said my hellos, smiled and kept moving. Arriving at the helicopter deck, I found the pilot stationed near the hangar, hosting guests and ensuring his precious airframes were not at risk from inquisitive hands. He waved me over and we walked to the rail at the edge of the deck. He motioned for me to look forward along the hull and as I was looking, he said, 'That's a bit close, isn't it?'

There was a smaller sailboat at anchor that was very close to the yacht, maybe 10 metres from the hull at the mid-point. Way too close. I thanked the helicopter pilot and was already moving to the bridge. The bridge was three decks above and quite a walk: I took the longer, though private, crew stairs two at a time.

I arrived breathless on the bridge and moved straight to the port bridge wing where I could look back towards the sailboat. In a break with my normal practice, I did not initially seek the officer of the watch stationed on the bridge. The sailboat remained 10 metres from the hull, and still a danger. My thoughts were: 'Make safe first and fill in details second.' Taking control on the bridge wing, I looked to the sensors and noted that due to a wind shift and a failure of one of the satellite positioning units, our yacht had moved 70 metres from her original safe position and we remained dangerously close to the smaller boat. The sailboat was already anchored when we arrived and the obligation was upon us to keep away. I reset our yacht's dynamic positioning system, which renewed our satellite position, then reset the wind sensor and returned the yacht to the original position, away from the sailboat.

My actions only took 40 seconds, but that is a long time to have not seen the officer of the watch. My taking control had set off an on-screen alert on the bridge and still he hadn't come to see what was going on. The starboard side of the bridge was 24 metres away and obscured by the last golden rays of light to the west, streaming through the windows. I shielded my eyes to see and then heard the officer of the watch being photographed with and fawned over by four Victoria's Secret models. Trying not to sound too terse, I called him over from his new-found friends. The models continued to pose for each other, with champagne flutes held high, well-practised distant looks, tilted hips and pursed lips.

I was ready to really tear him up for his lack of attention and for allowing photography on the yacht in breach of privacy agreements. As he walked the 12 metres to join me at the centreline, I could see his sheer happiness being displayed in a truly imbecilic grin. He was an awkward 25-year-old man and the idea of being the centre of attention of four of the most beautiful women on the planet had left him less than useless to fulfil his safety obligations. I couldn't berate someone in this state, so instead I pointed out the steps I had taken to keep the yacht in position and maintain safety. His face changed with the awareness of how close it was to an accident and he rejoined me from his stupor: he was truly sorry. I smiled it off, saying it was all OK, nothing happened, no foul. I said quietly, 'Enjoy the experience with the guests but do so without forgetting why you are actually here.'

He nodded meekly as one of the models joined us to see what held our attention. The bridge officer and I were still both looking down towards the sailboat. The model heard me speak and excitedly introduced herself as a fellow Australian, raised in a rural town I knew only by its remoteness and it being a synonym for a 'hard-up place'. In that moment, I realised she must have relied on her intelligence far more than her beauty to have lifted herself from a life among Australia's rural disadvantaged. We saw each other then: the supermodel and the superyacht captain, and with a moment of clarity saw how our lives could have been very different. I let the moment pass and with a firm grip on the forearm of the officer of the watch, I smiled at the ladies and gave them an instruction: 'Keep an eye on him, he's an important guy keeping us all safe.' One of the models mock-saluted me and they all giggled as I departed.

I entered the guest area from the back of the bridge and as I reached the main stairwell, I heard the gentle Italian-accented English of Gio, the submarine pilot from the deck below. He was still giving the tour. As I came down the stairs to the lower landing, I saw him recounting to a group of five the history of a magnificent maritime relic that was displayed there. The Hollywood director saw me first and smiled, and as he and I separated from the bigger group to view the cinema, he turned to me and said, 'I really should make a film about you and about all this.' My response came out more swiftly than was probably appropriate (this is a lifelong failing and something I keep working on, without success): 'You can't afford the production costs, and nobody would believe you.' I realised what I had just said and flushed. To the credit of this wonderful artist, he smiled broadly, nodded in agreement and we entered the cinema.

This frames the environment we are speaking of. Until space travel becomes a commercial reality, the yachts in this book are the greatest display of wealth on the planet. Equal to the yachts are the yacht owners, whose complexity rivals their yachts. My small role in this world is as their captain. From Homer to Ahab, there is a historical fascination with the role of the captain, and today the title 'Captain' brings with it a sense of expectation, a hoped-for competence.

A sense of maturity in thought and action. I shared this view in childhood and then through my career ascending towards this lofty ideal. I was not carrying a cargo or even passengers seeking their week's holiday. I, as the superyacht captain, was entertaining the wealthiest and most glamorous in the world. I was their host, their entertainer, sometimes their confessor and always their guardian. Yes, I could joke with the supermodels on the bridge and even endure their cheeky mocking, but I could never take my eye off the safety and efficiency of the operation.

Like many who set a goal and then spend a long time achieving it, my view from the captain's chair was very different from the one I had when I gazed upon it from a distance. I thought that, as a captain, my self-doubt would recede and through the power of the title my errors would decrease. Unfortunately, both increased. There were times when an observer might perceive from my manner – trying to be the captain I had long wanted to be – a confidence bordering on arrogance. It wasn't. Any outward show of confidence was my placing a shield between what I was really feeling and what was visible. I want people to realise that most positions they might aspire to are held by people who don't think they deserve to be there either. They might just be better at hiding it. My journey is not one of ever-increasing competence in response to circumstance; it is often a scared boy just holding on. Another goal of this book is to pull the curtain back on how fine the line is between success and failure, safety and catastrophe. This is my lived truth, but I think it is far more common than many 'leader's memoires' would have readers believe.

Nobility of purpose

There is a gorilla in the room throughout my yachting career. What is the nobility of purpose when I speak of yachts in the hundreds of millions, operating budgets in the tens of millions and guests flying around the world in private jets to join them for the sole purpose of leisure?

'Nobody needs a yacht.'

This was said by Jon Bannenberg, one of the most influential of modern yacht designers. If even he is saying this, what hope do I have of justifying my chosen career in the face of environmental concerns and a world challenged by gaping wealth disparity? I am not here to defend yachting, but nor am I going to allow yachting to stand at the whipping post when the global community finds a conscience.

Although I don't lean too heavily on the 'trickle-down economics' defence that is often used with yachting, there are thousands of jobs at sea and ashore reliant on yachts. Normal people, working each day to live and support their families, to develop skills and to grow through their careers. Additional to the people are the yachts themselves. Yachts are the leading edge of technological innovation at sea, a chance to try non-commercially viable projects that in time may improve the efficiency of global shipping. The Formula 1 of the seagoing community.

Sitting atop the yachts and those that work within them are the billionaires funding the adventure. All those I have supported in my career undertake philanthropy and legacy projects. These may involve the environment, social justice, medical research or more. They rarely, if ever, seek media recognition for these projects. I worked for an English billionaire who retained two medical researchers for the sole purpose of reviewing the submissions he received for funding. Another tech billionaire funded the 'Oscars of Science' to promote academic excellence. Yet another funds the world's largest marine protected area.

One yacht I had the privilege to command was very capable, carrying large boats with cranes of up to 20 tonnes. After a hurricane hit the outer Bahamas, the yacht's owner released his craft for several weeks to support disaster relief efforts: we saved lives and helped a vanquished community get back on their feet with essential supplies. The only provision from the yacht owner was that it was to be done anonymously. Likewise, with another yacht in the Indian Ocean, we supported Stanford University's Marine Science Station. The crew and I tagged more sharks than ever before in the history of this large ocean. The data from this project moved marine biologists forward a decade from their previous goals.

I have had many life and career inflections and maybe I could have delivered more to the global good if I had never stepped on a superyacht, but I did, and I am proud that I did.

What do you give?

Shake your head at the excess if you must, but also think: in our own lives, how much do we give back to science, the arts, the environment?

Maybe we do not have the millions to spare, but do we give our time, our support?

Part One

MY JOURNEY: BEFORE THE CAPTAIN WAS THE BOY

You can have the shoes

I was a shy, bookish boy and I lived in a small Western Australian coastal town. By age 11 I was a little overweight, and the last to be picked for any team sports. Fortunately, a growth spurt during my 12th year helped me climb the sports social ranking, but I always carried the shadow of those days when I was the 'clever little fat kid'. It shaped my outlook, always a little on the outside and not quite expecting to be chosen. I would never have thought that I would one day be at ease with the wealthiest people on the planet and that I would feel more at home in Monaco, Geneva, St Barths, Moscow and London than I did returning to my home town.

My idyllic childhood was spent between home in Rockingham and school in Fremantle, Western Australia. Rockingham was an 'anywhere Australia' coastal town that began as a country respite for farmers and in time developed into a feeder town for nearby industries. My childhood spanned the 1970s to mid 1980s – a time when drinking from the warm garden hose was a treat, and sunburnt skin and a peeling nose were of no concern – Rockingham suffered from the normal social tensions of the age but was 'mostly harmless'. These days are hued by time, but I remember them fondly. I often refer to my childhood by reference to the much-loved Australian author Tim Winton, who writes of sandy homes and sandy people where children fish, ride bikes and mess around in boats. There is rarely wealth on show in his wonderful stories: the Winton characters are working men and women who live through their share of adversity. The cars are worn, the homes and the people bent by the elements. This was my childhood, and great material wealth did not make the screenplay.

My father worked hard for the family. He was an older parent, born during the depression years into an Irish Catholic immigrant family of six children where, like so many from this time, there was never anything to be spared. He had served in Rabaul, Papua New Guinea during the final years of the Second World War and in a nod to an Australian cliché he rarely, if ever, referred to the war years. Even by the time of his passing, when I was 24 years old and also serving in the navy, I had never learned anything about that period of his life.

My father's stories of childhood were framed by frugality. Children worked in support of the family, bathing was a privilege and always shared, meat was a rare luxury, and clothes were always repaired, resewn and handed around. To break free from this cycle, my father relied on an uncanny affinity with numbers. In his early teens, he spent time at the horse races and became the 'pencil' for a bookmaker. This skill makes little sense today, but in an era before automated calculation my father constantly summed numbers and reworked the odds to allow the bookmaker to take bets from gamblers. When, by age eight, I too could add a column of numbers at the speed it takes to read them, I was a parlour novelty for my parents and somewhat nervous that I too might be sent to the track to pay my way.

My numeracy was never tested at the track, as through application and hard work my father broke free of the Irish immigrant curse and my sister and I were raised in Australian middle-class comfort. We had tennis lessons, my mother being a former tennis professional, went to horse-riding camps, and I was always at the yacht club looking for someone to sail with. We enjoyed the trimmings of a coming-of-age Australia; life was a Reg Mombassa palette, and the coast was the canvas.

I was of a generation where the refrain 'children should be seen and not heard' was said often. This gave many freedoms; the helicopter parent was probably 15 years away from their first flight, and my sister Tracey and I were free to (mostly) do as we pleased. Being three years my senior, Tracey guided our days, and her tastes shaped my earliest memories. Tracey read quality literature voraciously and listened to Elvis and The Beatles. I look to her now as being retro before there was a term to describe seeking pleasure in tradition and quality.

In my pre-teen years I met Michael, another young beachside vagrant. He was a little different in that he was the local doctor's son. He had a bit of style at a young age and excitingly lived in a house where his parents had an en suite, introducing a level of wealth I had not seen before. This was 1970s Australia, en suites were not common, and in fact I did not know the word for a bathroom in the bedroom. We became inseparable friends throughout our childhood: we dived, fished, rode our bikes and just enjoyed being boys. I was amazed by how open his family was: sex, politics and more were all shared at the dinner table (a table where I was always welcome) and their influence has had a large part to play in my life. I have written various letters of thanks over the years, some duplicating the ones before, but none shall truly repay the debt of gratitude I have for another family doing nothing more than telling a formerly overweight little kid that 'you can do anything'.

One afternoon, Michael and I were cleaning up our mess of dive and fishing equipment at his home, and I saw in a tea chest on the front porch a pair of new running shoes. Running shoes were more than a commodity; they were social currency, social identity. I recognised the pair as being one of the most sought after of the time: Reebok, new to Australia. I asked Michael about the shoes, and he said they were his, but he had forgotten about them. If I wanted, I could take them. I could not have been more shocked. Who has a spare pair of new trainers that they do not remember? Within my own context, I had stumbled across some serious wealth. I returned home that night to do some readjusting. In my future I would meet families with personal staff into the hundreds and property portfolios valued at hundreds of millions of dollars, yet through it all that extra pair of running shoes remains with me to this day as a symbol of excess.

In parallel to this friendship, I was playing football (Australian Rules Football) for the local club, the not so creatively named Rockingham Rams. This was a different group to any I had experienced before: they came from 'Rockingham Park', and many were children of the English workers who had immigrated to Australia for the heavy industrial area of Kwinana. They were tougher than me, they were tougher than my school friends and they were worlds away from my summer friend Michael. Nevertheless, they took me in; they accepted me as I stepped off the school bus in a school uniform and tie. They accepted that I spoke of university, whereas at 12 years old they were already waiting to work in the industrial complex of their parents' experience.

All these differences aside, I felt a true sense of belonging with this group. We moved through the years of junior football together and I watched as some left football to work, and others had run-ins with the law. Tragically, one of the more talented boys died in a fight with his brother. In coastal Australia, sometimes it ended that way. This duality felt natural. I felt no conflict between having dinner with the wealthiest family in the area on a Saturday and playing football with the children of struggling families on a Sunday. At times the two worlds collided, and I revelled in being able to step between them.

There was a shopping mall that on a Thursday had evening trading. For a 14-year-old looking for first love it was the place to see and be seen, but it was not without risk. The mall was beset by youth gang violence, and to get a beating in the car park for no apparent reason was not uncommon. More than once, I realised I was being given safe passage through the guardianship of my teammates from the football club. More extraordinary was that Michael was granted the same. One evening, Michael and I were walking through the underpass that led below the main road and away from the shopping centre. It was dark and the four loitering youths backlit by the street light would have looked ominous even if they were choirboys. Michael with his misplaced confidence, his swagger and expensive clothing set them on edge.

We were 20 paces from the group in the confines of the tunnel when a 16-year-old with long ginger hair, a youthful scraggy beard, acne and a strength in his build that belied his youth stepped forward squarely into our path. I am not naturally confident, and my instinct was to turn and run.

He gave the expected greeting: 'Piss off or we're gonna smash you.' Michael, always the leader, said in a low voice, 'Keep walking', so I did. We were backlit from the shopping centre and, as they were to us, we were only silhouettes to the youths. It was getting to the point of no return when Long-haired said, 'It's Bren! How are you, mate?' I mumbled a broken-voiced response as he said to the others, 'You know him, quick, wears number 22 for the under 14s,

7

the posh kid from the city school.' There was some nodding of agreement as Michael and I passed through. As we were leaving the danger zone of the underpass, the voice called out, 'See you at training on Tuesday, Bren!' In a voice lacking any conviction, I called back, 'Su-ure, great.'

Somewhere through this, I realised the power of being able to move between worlds and to be the unseen connector within them.

The time stamp of your home town always stays with you, even long after it stops being a feature in your life. In 2014 I was in Monaco to meet colleagues and, through unconnected paths, three children of Rockingham were also staying in the Fairmont Hotel. The chances of this defy any logic, the Fairmont being a world-class hotel and Rockingham being, well, anything but. Michael's elder sister Lisa (on whom, truth be told, I had had an unrequited crush for most of my teen years) was one of this group. The champagne flowed as fast as the stories, some hilarious and some tragic – not all from our childhood made it out of the cultural wilderness of coastal Australia and not all made it to adulthood. At several points through an increasingly raucous evening, we all shook ourselves down with the realisation that four urchins from Rockingham, Western Australia were ordering champagne in Monaco.

What's 'porn' in Russian?

The morning after the night in the Fairmont, I meekly joined my colleagues in the Monaco Yacht Club. I knew it was going to be a very long day and it was such amateur form to be starting it with minimal sleep and a hangover. We had met to conduct a pre-meeting rehearsal before we took the helicopter to Nice airport for the Aeroflot flight to Moscow. We were presenting to a client the technical details supporting a €300 million yacht that was soon to begin construction.

After the always tortuous path through Russian customs, we met our handlers for the trip to the private residence of the client. On arrival at the walled compound, we were subject to electronic and physical security checks that stopped just short of a prostate exam. Once through, we were accompanied by translators, private staff and guardians as we walked to a large meeting room in an outer building. We laid out the plans, documents and electronic drawings and we waited, and waited.

Some hours later the client joined, and we presented late into the night and the next morning. It was an epic project, and the client's team was drilling for details. Thankfully, my co-presenter was a garrulous chief engineer from New Zealand and she led the meeting, reciting fact after fact in response to relentless challenges. The questions were not important for the success of the project, they were important for *our* success. The client's team wanted to know that we knew everything in microscopic detail. Aside from my colleague's competence, my only other saviour was the time needed to translate each question from Russian to English and back. As it neared 3am, I was fading; I had lost count of the espresso coffees I had consumed in the last 20 hours and just hoped this interrogation was going to end soon. Just 24 hours earlier I was talking of long afternoons at Palm Beach jetty and toasting with champagne to a carefree childhood. Also in my thoughts was that the return flight to France was boarding at 9am. With customs and Moscow's infernal traffic, I knew we were going to go straight through. Why had I even checked in to the hotel?

With eyes heavy and mind wandering badly, I was brought back to the room by the client demonstratively asking in Russian why there was no USB port adjacent to his bed that would feed the television in the master suite. Following translation, the audio-visual consultant took over, presenting with some condescension why there was no need for this. All entertainment would be streamed and there would be no need for such an antiquated approach as a USB port.

The client was tired too, getting louder and clearly not happy. It was also apparent that he understood English perfectly. Cutting through the escalating noise, my engineering colleague, with her eyes firmly on the oligarch, asked the translator, 'So how do you say "porn" in Russian? He wants to watch his own porn.'

The oligarch client stood, laughed, shook our hands, and hugged Sarah, the engineer. Without another word, he departed: we had passed the test and won the contract. Sarah could not have found Rockingham on a map, but that morning in Moscow I bestowed on her honorary home-town status.

There is no second place

Returning to childhood, Michael's tutelage guided me through adolescence. We were 'mostly' good kids and life was following the script of a coastal Australian town when in 1987 the America's Cup came to Fremantle. The America's Cup is a yacht race like no other and it was a transformative event for me, for Fremantle, for Australia – and it was all thanks to the vision of the enigmatic entrepreneur Alan Bond. In 1983, in Newport, Rhode Island, he had wrestled the trophy, the Auld Mug, from the grasp of the United States for the first time in 132 years. The prime minister, Bob Hawke, famously announced an impromptu public holiday in a television address, while holding a beer and wearing an Australian flag sports jacket. Australia stopped and then made its way to the bars and clubs to celebrate. The win galvanised the nation and, in many ways, marks the moment Australia entered the world stage.

The America's Cup is more than a yacht race; it is theatre. It has victory, defeat, skulduggery, underdogs, titans, warriors, heroes and villains. In Fremantle, the names were in the news daily: Connor, Murray, Bertrand, Lexcen, Bond and many more. The Australian symbols were the Boxing Kangaroo flags, which flew everywhere, and the band Men at Work's hit song 'Land Down Under', which played all day every day on every radio and street speaker. Alan Bond, then considered our greatest hero, will be forever shadowed by his convictions for corporate crimes, including the stranger than fiction fraudulent purchase of Vincent van Gogh's painting *Irises*. This had yet to play out in 1987, and for me he is the one to thank for transforming my home town and shaping my life.

Before the America's Cup, Fremantle was a workers' town where the ports, the abattoir, the tanning sheds and the hotels were the dominant cultural – and in the case of the tanning sheds, sensory – touchpoints. There was a marina, and it was filled with fishing boats. To see the town today with its dining, café culture, music scene, bustling tourist economy, gentrified homes and port developments, you would never believe where it came from and the difference one yacht race and one man's vision could make. The same is true for my own life: if it were not for this event, my life may have been more about tanning sheds and hotels and less about sunsets in Bora Bora.

The America's Cup coincided with my final school exams, and it took quality reframing of the facts to convince my parents it was a good idea for me to take on part-time work while attending school. Fortunately, they valued work above anyone's chosen God, and I was permitted to apply. I took a part-time job at The Esplanade, the hotel most central to the event. The Esplanade was ground zero for the post-race action and where all the actors of this yachting theatre moved. That I was working there was just too incredible for my juvenile mind to comprehend.

The job advertised was window cleaning, general yard duties and pool attendant. I applied myself to these tasks, but I quickly found that so long as I worked hard, I could go wherever and do whatever I wanted. I roamed the large hotel just 'plugging in' where I was most needed. Sometimes it was the front bar, sometimes the pool, but wherever I chose it was the busiest and involved the greatest number of guests. I was given a cleaner's uniform, with a blue smock coat and trousers. I explained to the house manager that, due to the nature of the America's Cup, it would look more appropriate if I wore a white polo shirt, beige shorts and boat shoes. Somehow, she agreed; it was my first experience of shaping the workplace to my wishes and, without knowing, I had just designed my first yacht uniform.

With school, sports and work, I had a busy schedule. At the hotel I had access to a night janitor's sleeping room that was not in use and I turned it into my study. I kept my bicycle in there too and would sleep at the hotel a couple of times a week when I finished late and had school the next morning. Even with this tight schedule, I found time to explore the newly completed Royal Perth Yacht Club Annexe and the transformed fishermen's harbour. There were yachts larger and more diverse than had ever sailed the Western Australian coast. On them there were men and women in matching uniforms, including racers, cruisers and those who really knew nothing about sailing but were happy to be associated with the event. I was hooked.

I saw that this was a community I could belong to. Working on a boat made sense to me and at 17 years old

I started talking to those in crew uniforms about how to 'get started' in yachting. Yacht owners I met around the hotel recognised a youthful energy and said that when I finished school, I should look them up. When I was handed business cards, I stared at the array of numbers for the international phone listings and the complicated addresses. The world was getting a lot bigger, and fast.

I was ready to speak to my conservative parents and share this new idea of joining a yacht to 'sail away' and had almost forgotten that, between clearing tables at The Esplanade, I had applied to join the Royal Australian Navy. The navy offered an allowance to finish school and then undertake military and academic studies at the recently opened Australian Defence Force Academy. So as Australia sank deep into recession, a paid university degree and guaranteed employment was too much to ignore, despite my new-found passion for the yachting community. I did not know very much about the navy and still less about this new Defence Academy, but I would soon learn about both very quickly. Thirty days after finishing school I boarded only the second flight in my life and flew the five hours from Perth to Canberra. I had met quite a few other applicants during the rounds of testing at the Defence Recruiting Centre in Perth, but boarding the plane there were just four of us. I would later find out that only 5 per cent of the applicants were accepted and, given that the recession only worsened in subsequent years, it was one of the wisest, if least well informed, decisions I would ever make.

To lead to excel

The Australian Defence Force Academy was a bold and insightful concept, even if the details of how it would operate were not quite worked out at the time of opening. There must have been many planning meetings and I have often wondered why nobody was empowered to ask, 'What do you think 800 overachieving 18 to 21-year-old men and women, all housed together, receiving an income, a long way from parents, and with little oversight, could possibly get up to?' It wasn't asked and in consequence we had a blast; we made incredible friendships and along the way received some top-flight education from both our university lecturers and the military staff.

At my small school in Fremantle, I stood out: school captain, one of the top academic students and athletics champion year after year. In Canberra, I was surrounded by the top 5 per cent and I just was not in the game. Their excellence was apparent in academia, sport, social awareness and, well, everything I was lacking. My shortcomings were brought out daily, some visible to all and some just to me. In either case, I knew I was only holding on by a thread to keep up with this new peer group.

The first six weeks of training had passed in a blur of fatigue, running to and from meaningless destinations and constant bastardisation. To mark its completion and the commencement of the academic year, there was a sports event known as 'Lawn Lap' – a release from the endless formal routines, where the six squadrons, each of around 120 cadets, fielded their two best runners. With past successes over similar distances, I somehow had the gumption to nominate myself as one of these runners. It was a festive day, and all were proud to be there. A significant number of cadets had already resigned within these first weeks, too confronted by institutional life. Those of us remaining were buoyant and proud: it was a very small step on a long path, but it was something. Those not running in the event enjoyed champagne on the bleachers surrounding the parade ground, converted for the day to a sprint track. Looking at the racecourse I was confident, and fully expected to win by a streak. I hadn't been beaten over 400 metres since the age of 13, when I had shed my childhood weight.

There were twelve runners representing the six squadrons and we each wore our colours. My squadron, Charlie, wore US school-bus yellow. We looked to the stands and could clearly see our friends also decked in squadron colours. The atmosphere was beyond anything I had experienced and indulgently I felt as though I was a cast member in the film *Chariots of Fire*. I started strongly, and on the first corner I turned within the lead group. I really felt I was going to keep this position, but with the sheer quality of the runners there was never a chance. By the home straight I was gasping for breath at 80 metres behind the lead group – the same runners I had been on the shoulders of, 600 metres and four corners earlier.

The winner was a further 40 metres ahead of the main group and accelerating at the same pace I was slowing. I could feel my head craning to the sky and my stride shortening in a pose often struck by the last-place holder in the junior school races. I crossed the line and was cheered and supported as though I was the winner. This camaraderie was nothing I had known before, and it was intoxicating. Later, in the midst of the champagne, the laughs and the release of six weeks of torment, I realised that in this 'wider world out there', as soon as I felt near the top it would always shift and I would have to work harder. I had found a place I belonged, but I needed to work harder than I ever had before: despite their unconditional friendship, my classmates were a talented bunch.

The three years at the Defence Academy were a bit raucous, a bit indulgent and at all times shaped by a well-intentioned ignorance of anything but our own needs. We studied for our exams and outside of this we were schooled in military history, protocols of the service we had joined, leadership and personal development. Like so much in life, the two topics I found least relevant at the time – leadership and personal development – are the two that have served me so well through a life leading and being led.

The obligation placed against the fully funded degree was to serve one year in the service for every year under training and then one in addition (for the Queen). I took to the travel and the lifestyle of a young naval officer with relish. It was before the Australian military took itself too seriously and we sailed and conducted warfare drills, all with the aim of reaching the next cocktail party. It was a great time, but I could see that my enjoyment horizon was limited when I looked to those more senior than I, who were focused on the administration and not the raucous fun I was living as a junior.

In 1997, I fondly bade farewell to the navy; I felt all the fun belonged to the juniors and if I stayed any longer it was about to get serious. I had also never let go of my first unrequited love, the one I met during the America's Cup: yachting. To step towards my dream, I took up sailing full time to determine whether a professional ocean-racing career could be in my future. I raced: in Australia with Sydney to Hobart campaigns, in the UK at Cowes and in Fastnet campaigns, and even on a short-lived, ill-fated America's Cup team. I learned I was a solid yachtsman, but to make it as a professional ocean racer takes a level of focus and commitment that was above what I was ready to deliver. I had to think of something else.

The tuck and tape

With not much else as a fallback, I looked to something with moral virtue to apply myself to; sailing is wonderful, but maybe I had something more noble to give. I moved to Darwin to attend the Northern Territory University, studying for a graduate diploma in Aboriginal education. I thought I had something to offer as an educator: my own schoolteachers were caring and had made a difference to my life, so maybe I could do the same for others? Above this, the navy had prioritised communications as a virtue and joining childhood experience with professional competence seemed to make sense. The worthiest in the Australian community of receiving this education were and remain the Aboriginal people. It just felt right.

The education at Northern Territory University was wonderful. I enrolled as a middle-class white Southern Australian raised in state-endorsed ignorance of the needs of the most disadvantaged group in Australia, and by the end of the first semester I had become an advocate for a solution to the 'Aboriginal problem'. A problem that would prove elusive to successive state and federal governments to define, let alone address, competently. I resented that my Anglo-Australian education had not even scratched the surface of the original sin of English Australia. Throughout my schooling, only lip service had been paid to the history and the reality of the modern indigenous Australians.

To fund the adventure, I held down two part-time jobs: one working at a bottle shop and the other at the Fannie Bay Yacht Club (yes, that's a real place). The two, alongside my studies, only allowed for a humble time financially, although – motivated by thoughts of becoming an educator in the Aboriginal community – I was very happy.

Darwin is different in many ways to Southern Australia. It is geographically closer to Asia than it is to the populated South of Australia and prides itself on its clichéd perception as a frontier town. Opportunity was around every corner and the network was so small that a career could be shaped from an evening at one of the many hotels, and this is precisely what happened. It seemed of little relevance to my world but the union-controlled waterfront was under attack from a reformist conservative federal government that sought to break the stranglehold on all things moving on and off Australian docks. The militant Maritime Union of Australia was having its back broken and the whole process was televised into the nation's houses with images of non-union labour being escorted to the docks shielded by balaclava-wearing, Rottweiler-commanding security guards. It was a confronting time for Australia, which more by luck than good judgement had ridden above the violence that other labour disputes had wrought around the world.

It seemed a long way from my daily routine of university, bottle shop and yacht club, but on a Friday night, at sunset drinks, one of the yacht club members (who was aware of my prior career as a naval officer) asked if I was just a yachtie, or if I was commercially qualified too.

At this time, naval service was not recognised and prior to leaving Western Australia I had completed further studies to gain the Master Class 4 skipper's licence. A low-order qualification in the scheme of things, but it was enough to skipper a harbour tug and it seemed that this is just what this yacht club member, who turned out to be linked to the large shipping conglomerate P&O Maritime, had in mind. He complimented me on my work ethic at the yacht club, and I thought no more of the conversation. I was surprised when two weeks later I was asked to attend an interview for a manager's role with P&O Maritime.

I met one of the senior P&O Maritime managers and while the detail of that interview has long passed from memory, his compulsive adjusting and grooming of his combover hasn't. It caught my eye once, twice, and then I lost count. The interview continued and I returned my thoughts from hair and the urge to snip the unruly tufts to focus on understanding his intent. The interview seemed to centre solely around ensuring that I held no contacts with the unionised waterfront. I confirmed this multiple times without needing to expand that I had not joined any union only because the opportunity had not presented itself. There weren't too many unions for off-the-books 'cash' labour at bottle shops and yacht clubs. We didn't discuss any of my skills, experience or values, which was just as well, as for skills and experience I would have drawn a blank and, at 27 years old, I was still working through my values. I knew the virtue of my studies, but I also realised this was a once in a career opportunity. I sensed the interview was merely a formality, as they so often are. So it was that in the beer garden of the Hyatt Hotel Darwin, like many things in the Northern Territory, the commitment to start working on the new non-unionised waterfront was consummated with a beer or more.

Sadly, sometimes an idealist is beaten by an economic reality. My studies were noble, and I was enjoying the personal growth, but as a manager/tug skipper, even non-union, I would be earning close to the income of the Darwin High School principal. I withdrew from the course and my own sense of withering to economic reward over moral virtue was reflected in the faces of the impassioned lecturers. They had seen my interest as a chance for their cause: I was a conservative white Australian who had overcome institutional ignorance and, like so many others, I had slipped away before delivering on the implicit promise of my studies. On a quiet day, I often find myself wondering whether I may have made a difference as a voice on behalf of an often-muted people.

I did not have time to contemplate, as within two days I was in Sydney, receiving a two-week cram course on tug work and harbour manoeuvring. Two weeks was not nearly enough, even with an excellent and ever patient instructor. Clive was well past retirement but was retained for the sheer depth of knowledge he held. It was clear that while he could wave the flag with the unionists or with the privatisation group, he was in the twilight of his career and making a stand in either direction was not worthwhile. After our introductions, he made sure I knew that even though he would put his full effort into my training, it wasn't right, and the 'suits' ran the risk of injuring or killing people on the harbour. I smiled and limped through an awkward response: it was squarely a point against my inexperience. Clive was correct, and in the rush to break the unions and privatise, corners were cut and there was no possible way to replace decades of experience in weeks. The unionised waterfront workers were disastrous to negotiate with, but they knew their work. I, on the other hand, had absolutely no idea.

Clive needed to airbrush the shortcomings in my knowledge. He would direct and I would control as we towed barges, connected to ships with long and short lines and moved around a busy harbour. After a week, my competence was growing, and Clive and the crew had warmed to my presence. I was no longer the symbol of waterfront reform; I was just a kid trying to learn and do the best he could. I was tired from the long days, which were as mentally exhausting as they were physically demanding. It was rare that I did not feel under direct assessment, and in addition to the training the tug also kept its schedule of 'real work' for the period. Connecting to a ship coming into Sydney Harbour at 8 knots is not for the faint-hearted. It goes against all sense of safe operations to drive towards the exposed hull of a ship in ballast. As I would often hear, tug driving is a contact sport.

We were nearing the completion of one of the longer days when Clive returned to the little wheel house and gave a simple request. 'Just tie up here. One line is fine and keep the engine engaged.' With a modest nod, I confirmed I would do as requested, and as I turned to speak I noticed that Clive had withdrawn to the small tea station at the rear of the wheel house. He had put the kettle on and was unwrapping what looked like a baked loaf from a neatly folded check cloth. I looked to the deck to see if one of the three other crew members was available to pass the line for me. It didn't register with any surprise, but the engineer was already standing with a line in his hand, ready to pass to the pontoon ashore.

The tug settled gently on the pontoon and without lifting his gaze from the tea, Clive asked, 'So tell me, what is significant about where we are?' I had been under assessment for close to two weeks and was ready for all of Clive's tutorials. My response was solid, and without a fumble, I ranged through tide, current, visibility and other harbour traffic. These were textbook answers and I was comforted that as I spoke Clive just smiled, stirred the teas and gently nodded his head. We were joined by the other crew and Clive handed each of us a cup of tea and then the date loaf that he had so carefully unwrapped and sliced. It was home-made by his wife, and it was clear the crew knew the quality of the bake and also Clive's attention to cleanliness, as they all took a paper towel to hold the slice, lest they scatter crumbs in the wheel house.

Drawing a breath after a sip of tea, Clive continued, 'This is a very important spot for all of us that work on the harbour and if you do return to Sydney, you must remember it. It is called overtime point.' The crew knew it was not their time to speak but their smiles and nods in unison added weight to Clive's words. Meekly, I responded, 'I won't forget, Clive, thanks, and I appreciate it.' We continued in relatively awkward silence for a few minutes and on Clive's cue the teacups were returned, and the engineer took over cleaning the little kitchenette. There was no communication on this routine; it was clear these roles had been defined for a long time.

Once the engineer left the wheel house, I asked Clive to explain in a little more detail what 'overtime point' meant, yet again exposing my naivety to the ways of the harbour. He smiled knowingly. I might have learned how to connect 'push-pull' to a ship coming into Sydney or tow 200-tonne barges along the Parramatta River, but I still had no idea, and never would, of the finer points of the waterfront culture. Clive explained with patience that the tug had been away from its berth for 7 hours and 15 minutes and we would have made it back to the berth by 7 hours and 30 minutes. The significance of this was still lost on me and my perplexed look showed the need for further explanation. The tug had docked on the rarely used north-facing ferry landing on Garden Island. A quiet spot in the otherwise busy Sydney Harbour that was on the way to the tug compound on the eastern side of the same island.

With a grin, Clive continued, 'This is one of the most important parts of your education...', and he went on to explain that 'overtime point' was an essential stop if the tug was ever passing by anywhere above six and a half hours' working. The significance was that working hours were defined by when the tug left and returned to the compound and if it were anywhere above eight hours all the crew would receive a double shift; 16 hours' pay with overtime loading. Clive was clear that to return the tug to the compound without thought to the overtime would shorten any tug skipper's career.

With this introduction to the ways of the Australian waterfront, I returned to Darwin. I had been given the grandiose title of 'Manager Northern Australia'. It sounded impressive when said in Sydney, but fundamentally it meant that when not skippering the tug and other harbour craft, I did the paperwork for the five staff from a dilapidated transportable hut adjacent to Larrakeyah harbour, which our civilian craft shared with naval patrol boats. Well, that is how it started… my five-person team would soon become forty and the few harbour craft expanded to my chartering any vessel that could be used to transport personnel and equipment in the harbour and later to East Timor.

My personal life changed too; I was freshly single and took an apartment in the newly developed Cullen Bay Marina. It was a wonderful apartment above a Japanese restaurant and opposite the best dining in Darwin at the time. I had already upscaled the office from the transportable hut to also being in Cullen Bay; we were now a shopfront office with a workshop. The tug and workboats were berthed in the protected waters of the marina, which we could walk to from the workshop. My work/life ecosystem was in place.

The last piece of the puzzle was coffee and luckily the best coffee in Darwin was also in this small corner of the bay.

The proprietor of the well-named Brave Café, Michael, was hilarious. He was openly gay, of Aboriginal descent and moved across all social circles with ease. I had two spare rooms and Michael took one as my flatmate. We could not have lived more different lives. I would rise early and work around the harbour and in the office until evening. Michael would wake late, take his shift at the café from lunch and then party well into the night. Most mornings the apartment was returned to being spotless after late-night soirées, the only evidence being the multiple empty champagne bottles (always Moët & Chandon or Veuve Clicquot) neatly arranged by the door as I departed for another long day. Sunday nights were drag queen nights at the café, something unprecedented in the rough and tumble of Darwin. The ladies used our apartment to dress, and while all were great company, I found that I learned more than I needed to and tended to seek the Sunday shifts on the tug to save my own embarrassment with the livingroom tuck-and-tape sessions prior to the show. Michael revelled in my conservative awkwardness and has done for decades since. I do not let people out of my life and when, many years later, Yvonne and I needed someone to support us, with my being at sea and two toddlers at home, Michael was our first call.

In Darwin, things were evolving. Exercise KAKADU is one of the largest defence exercises in Australia and the South Asian, Pacific region. I had asked the senior team in

Sydney whether I was permitted to approach the foreign military advance teams to offer our services and there was no objection, so I printed a series of flyers and handed them to the liaison officers at a barbecue I arranged on their behalf. I was not quite prepared for what happened next, but they all confirmed their requests for tugs, barges, crew transfer boats and for the fuel barge. In what seems to repeat again and again in my life, I was so far out of my depth that I did not even realise it at the time, and just expanded operations to meet demand. There was no schedule of fees available, so I made one up using a hash of what I thought was fair and what the visitors would find acceptable. Very quickly, the humble Darwin office became the highest revenue and gross profit centre in the company.

Our core team, the fabulous five, took this as a point of pride, but we didn't make these numbers for long before the Sydney management all came to visit. The CFO, the operations manager and finally the managing director all came to Darwin. What they found was a small group that had little time for corporates and just wanted to get the job done. The corporates were not impressed with the lack of deference they and their bureaucratic ways received during their visits. This might have ended badly for me, but just as the scope of supply for Exercise KAKADU was tapering, the East Timor liberation was beginning, and Darwin was the staging point for the constant stream of military and civilian support vessels being supplied by the Australian government. We continued in much the same manner as before and adapted to the new normal of Darwin being an important centre for maritime activities in Australia.

As exciting as the time was in Darwin, I was just another southerner passing through, and I had been campaigning for a transfer to Sydney for some time. It felt that so long as Darwin was performing above all realistic expectations, there would be little more than lip service paid to my requests, and I would need to find my own path 'back down south'.

Those first days working in Darwin Harbour were an enormous leap from all my previous experience and every day I seemed to be running ahead of an ever-flooding tide. It may seem a long way from superyacht captaincy, but I have drawn upon the experiences on and off the water in Northern Australia often in my yachting career and in my life's meanderings.

Learnings from the North

When you are out of your depth, it will strengthen not weaken you to ask for help from those you lead and those you report to.

You may have some fresh ideas and be the 'person of the moment', but there are many moments and your time will pass quickly.

When circumstance falls in your favour, take the opportunity with humility: it will be taken just as easily as it was given.

How much for the flag?

O ne of the key clients throughout KAKADU and East
Timor was a ship's agent – Chris, a director within a
shipping firm – who held defence contracts with the foreign
navies; his bookings contributed greatly to the significant
growth of the Darwin office. We had built a friendship based
on our mutual need for efficient delivery of services to shared
clients, and we recognised each other as being the type to 'get
on and do it'. What I did not know was that Chris and one other
were working, in addition to the agency roles I knew them
for, on tendering for what at the time was the largest defence
support contract ever awarded. In contrast to the other large
defence contractors, they did not assign a large team to the
bid. Instead, it was written by two intelligent, savvy, roguish
larrikins from Sydney (one being Chris), who, after working on
the road, had then holed up in a hotel room for a week to build
a comprehensive bid to secure the multi-year supply contract.
I would not learn of this until it was announced that he had
been successful, in a commercial coup of the highest order. It
shocked the contracting community that this enormous tender
could be won by 'two fellas and a card table'.

The true architect of this coup was a parody of the
archetypal Australian. He drank, smoked, laughed loudly
and was incredibly quick-witted. Chris was a 'road warrior'

ahead of his time and even though access to the internet was via dial-up modems from hotel room phones, he was a wizard in communicating at all hours from all destinations. The term 'bootstrap' had yet to be coined and 'start-up' related to engines not business, but Chris was living it all the same. I do not recall him ever making me a job offer. It was more a direction that I would join him and look after all port logistics for the Asia-Pacific region. He said he already had a food guy, and I knew harbour services and the client: we were away. In the first six months I travelled across Australia, Fiji, Vanuatu and Singapore, with an extended period in Hawaii.

I was running around with bags of cash (literally – bags of cash) paying for ship visits and writing invoices on the flight to the next ship. In Suva, Fiji, I conspicuously walked the main street with US$40,000 in a satchel, threading my way through rioters as a coup, one of several that marked the period, was beginning. In Vietnam, a street vendor set up adjacent to the ship, preparing 400 hotdogs. It smelt wonderful: just a shame that the order placed was for bread, with the description, 'hot-dog-style buns'. In Vanuatu I rented four flatbed trucks to tie the ship's lines around after noticing, two hours before the patrol boat was due to arrive, that the cast-iron bollards needed to secure them had been stolen, presumably sold as scrap.

The Australian navy were the core of the contract but the 'off-contract' work for the US and other navies was where the money was to be made. Chris had known this at the time of writing the tender and it was one of the major reasons he had won the bid ahead of the more evolved competition. We were operating at a loss on the core contract but making such an incredible profit on off-contract work that it did not matter.

To give a flavour of these times, one off-contract sale involved the visit of the USS *Kitty Hawk* aircraft carrier and accompanying battle group. The advance team were discussing their orders and, in a time when bottled water was not an everyday product in Australia, had requested three 330ml bottles, per man, per day. This seemed a fair request and to ensure I had the order correct I asked the liaison officer to confirm the numbers. He went through the ships that would be in port and where we were to place the water stations. There would be 7,000 crew for ten days. He hastened to add that he would not expect to pay more than A$1 per bottle. It wasn't until after the meeting that I realised I had just committed to supplying 210,000 bottles of water and I had no idea where to find them or how much they would cost. A few calls while driving back to the office and I had located a bottler in Western Sydney who could fill and deliver the entire order. The bottler said he would need to add two cents delivery charge to each bottle, taking it to 13 cents a bottle. He also offered to place recycling bins next to the bulk stations, at no cost. A good day's work.

For the same visit, one of the headline items was a large Australian flag to be hung adjacent to the large Stars and Stripes for the official reception. A very reasonable request, and I asked the liaison officer to define 'large'. He looked at his notes and said, '30 feet across the top would be about right'.

A quick metric conversion and I realised that a 10-metre-long flag would not be on the shelf. I could not think of where I could turn, so I rang my colleague, the 'food guy'. A laconic, country Queensland-raised Australian, he responded with a one-word answer – 'Westfield' – and then he rang off. It made sense: the shopping centres flew these enormous flags to attract suburban Australians from miles around. I rang the marketing manager at the large shopping centre in Western Sydney and asked if I could borrow a flag. From her tone it was clear she found it unusual, but she had one still in its wrapping and so long as I returned it, she thought it would be OK. I felt it wasn't quite confirmed, so I invited her to join me at the official cocktail party for the US Navy, and the deal was struck. The reception was held, the manager attended, the flag flew and the special relationship between the US and Australia continued. The US had paid US$4,000 for the flag, which was a lot less than their expectations, and were grateful that I took it back so they would not need to store it before their next visit. It was back in the office at Westfield on Monday morning.

These were exciting days, but I was not getting any closer to a yachting career that I felt was past due. I was buying the big glossy *Boat International* magazine for A$16 and savouring each page. I didn't understand all the narrative around the industry, but I just loved the photos of those beautiful yachts. I even tried out how it might feel to already be working in yachting... During one ship support tour, I visited a hairdresser I had never seen before and likely never would again. I indulged myself and the hairdresser with a story that I already worked on the superyachts – not to lie, but to see how the narrative felt to me. A queer thing to do looking back, but it felt right talking as yacht crew and it strengthened my resolve. I had to change direction soon.

In addition to this yearning, the wild ways of ship support lacked the structure I had always lived within. Up until this point I had always worked within the framework of a large organisation. Even in the craziest growth period of Darwin, I knew the parent firm were out there somewhere. Writing now, I cannot believe how difficult I found it to cope with the freedom a freewheeling leader provided me. I was a long way from discovering the power of working with tight objectives and only loose guidance, and I was not aware of this approach to leadership. Chris's objective was clear: 'Always over-serve the client', and his guidance vague: 'Make sure you turn a profit on every invoice that matters.' I should have stayed with Chris. He was freewheeling, but he was true. True to the client and we were true to ourselves.

Freedom and opportunity

Freedom is a word overused and rarely understood. Possibly the only thing more frightening than having freedom removed is having it given.

I received wonderful leadership that gave me the space to grow, yet I was not ready to fill the space given to me. Opportunity is only half the story; it is always opportunity at the right time that matters.

Greed is good

If I didn't know what truth in business did and did not feel like, I was about to find out.

I was somewhere looking after a ship, and I took a phone call from a friend I knew from my time in Darwin. Emma was attractive and we had made a good couple when we were seen around Darwin town, if only it were so. We'd run together several times a week and, beyond some enjoyable conversations, that was the extent of the relationship (this wasn't for want of my trying to extend to romance, I might add, but it was unrequited). Luckily, Emma was a good runner, and I was and remain an ugly but relatively efficient jogger, so we shared good pace, distance and conversation.

It was nine months since I had left Darwin and I was surprised when Emma called to say her father wanted to meet me. My first question was, 'Does he run too?' She said I was a clown and he wanted to talk to me about work. I knew Emma was from Queensland but beyond that I did not know too much of her family. I learned on the call that Emma's father was the founder of a significant firm in Brisbane's downtown and owing to my misplaced dissatisfaction with the lack of clear boundaries with the port logistics and agency adventures, I agreed to meet him. The appointment was an ordeal, with assistants and dates being agreed and cancelled multiple times.

A lunch meeting was finally fixed, and wearing my only suit, ill-fitting and out of fashion, I entered the newest and shiniest building on Brisbane's riverfront and sheepishly introduced myself to the reception desk. It was the first time I had ever walked into a stock brokerage and besides not knowing what I was doing there, I didn't quite know what all the employees were doing there either. The receptionist may or may not have sensed my lack of awareness, but from her disdain with my presence I think it was the former. Within the office she definitely held seniority in years, and through her demeanour it seemed this same authority was applied to her role. Each of the young brokers passing by drew a sharp comment or rebuke from the desk dragon in heels.

After a few awkward minutes watching quite beautiful young men and women depart for lunch in groups, I was given the nod from reception that my appointment was to start. The first person I'd seen as poorly dressed as I was made his way towards me. He was barrel-chested, in his early fifties and had a mobile phone pressed to his ear. He did not break stride or make eye contact; a flick from his free hand instructed me to follow and we pushed through the glass doors and took the stairs to the lobby. I could only hear one side of his phone call and a growing curiosity/ alarm was building as to the topic. The side I could hear resembled, 'Fuck, really, aw fuck it, he is a stupid little prick. No for fuck's sake no, fuck me that's not good. Yes, fuck yes do that.' Even in Australia, this expletive-filled dialogue seemed bizarre and as I wondered what on earth and who was being spoken to, my question was indirectly answered when the call finished with: 'Thanks love, I will be home for dinner.'

As the Motorola phone flipped shut, Emma's dad finally acknowledged me. 'So Paddy, you shag my daughter or what?' In freefall, I responded honestly but with a horribly lame 'No, we only run together'. 'Whatever Paddy, I don't give a shit if you do or don't. She does run funny though?' I mumbled a nothing response. The tortuous five-minute walk with its awkward phone call and personal questions was over. We entered the restaurant, bypassing the maître d', and sat at a table that was kept free by convention. We ordered, we ate, and I listened. I was to move to Sydney and take over as the manager for a publicly traded, exchange-listed company that specialised in ship supply. My input to the conversation was minimal and as it had been in Darwin, my skills and experience were never questioned. In this instance, the only consistent line of questioning was loyalty. Would I be loyal to him and him alone in the face of any questioning? The reasoning for this did not seem overly weighty at the time and since I was conditioned, from childhood through the navy, to give loyalty to authority figures and institutions, answering 'yes' felt natural.

Lunch ran to A$108 for the two of us. I had never spent more than A$10 on lunch before and I was dazed as we separated. I was not completely clear on the 'what happens next' but I was sure things were soon to change, yet again. The phone rang the following morning: it was my front desk dragon in heels. She maintained her disdain for me, which I would come to learn was her default setting for all the youths in suits. I was directed to visit a nominated car dealership to collect a car: the dealer was expecting me and would show me a selection within an agreed budget. I was also to pack for Sydney. I awkwardly gave notice to Chris and, true to all my judgement of him, he took it with absolute good grace. I was too straight for the freedoms he afforded me, and he knew I needed to find somewhere that structured the workplace in a way that I would find familiar. If only I knew; Chris's team resembled the postal service for structure in comparison to where I was heading.

I received a further brief on arrival in Sydney. Emma's father had taken a majority stock position in a poorly performing ship supply company that probably should never have been listed in the first place. The one value point was that the firm owned significant freehold land in every port of Australia. My role was to allow and, if possible, accelerate the fall of the company so as to allow Emma's father to take ownership outright and strip the assets, selling the properties for great profit. I received a significant advance 'to settle in'.

I know, I know. It should have been clear, but honestly, I did not even suspect how illegal this was. It did not take long to see it was a business in advanced decay and likely would collapse if left untended, but just letting this happen felt wrong. I recruited some new staff, former navy colleagues, and we managed to reverse the decline. We won new contracts, streamlined process and began to firm up longer-term supply agreements. I had thrice-weekly calls to Brisbane and while these initiatives received a fair hearing, I was reminded there was a bigger strategy in place. Within two weeks of one of these calls where I spoke of the business's improvement, the bonded store where the cigarettes and alcohol were kept was broken into and a week's cash was taken at gunpoint from the office manager on her way to the bank. Both acts seemed to show an uncanny familiarity with the layout and process of the business, but who knows. The police did not find anything incriminating.

With these two events, any chance of business recovery was now finished; our will was broken and a rapid decline followed. My calls with Emma's father became more upbeat. The share price was soon to fall below ten cents and trading was suspended not long after, with the business virtually in freefall. I was promised a second, larger payment to further help with 'resettlement' to Sydney. My knowledge of corporate law had not significantly increased but something did not smell right. I was about to decline the second payment when I received a call: the man to whom I had pledged unreserved loyalty had suffered a cardiac event and passed away years ahead of his time.

My first thoughts were of self-pity: with full sympathies to Emma and her family, I was left alone in the middle of something that I didn't fully understand and the bits I did were not aligning with the values I had begun to define for myself. Nobody else knew about the arrangement; the publicly traded firm had folded and with no other option I started out on my own. I sought and won new business and I worked. I really worked. It was nothing during this time for me to arrive before five in the morning and leave at ten in the evening. Through the day I would look to win business, visit ships, drive a forklift and help pack deliveries. There were not enough hours in the day, and I just kept on pushing myself. I felt like I was a juggler and every week someone from the crowd would throw in another ball. My job was to learn how to keep going and keep smiling while all the time the pace and complexity increased. This seemed to work for a while, until one morning I felt like I could not rise from bed. I was not hungover, I had no physical illness, but I couldn't seem to get out of the bedroom. I called my assistant and said I was sick, but I was never sick and didn't think I was then. She was an older and wiser Indian woman, and she said that maybe a rest would help. I thanked her without understanding, but the next day I felt the same. I could not face the office.

I was living on the end of a wharf in Sydney with movie stars and national rugby stars as neighbours, but I felt very alone. I managed to get out of the apartment, walked through Sydney's botanical gardens and somehow found myself at the Castlereagh Street building where my competitor's offices were. I took the lift to their floor without thought and asked to see their founder. He was an older man of Greek descent, and a gentleman who saw me for the brash upstart I was. I took no heed of long-established relationships, and my directness showed disrespect to his European values. We met, and I shared that the business I had built since the collapse of the former publicly traded firm was his if he cared to make an offer. To add some urgency, I said it was an offer that would expire at the day's end, and with another night's sleep I would likely change my mind.

Mid-afternoon, I was still aimlessly strolling the city when the phone rang. My competitor's son (who was closer in age to me) asked if I was serious, and I said I was. He made an offer of a sum that I accepted without fully hearing it: it was lower than the value of the company, but it would be payable in 28 days and as far as could be guaranteed, none of the 13-person team would lose their jobs. He said there was only one caveat: the sale contract would state I could not compete for two years, and I would need to stay on with an expense account for six months to introduce my clients. My answer: 'Where do I sign?'

For the next six months I introduced my clients, who did not really want to do business with the new owners but enjoyed lunch. I had banked the low sale price and the business continued, not at the pace I had set, but the jobs of the workers seemed safe. Some old practices had returned, with commissions being paid and multiple competing quotes being sent on different letterhead from the same office, but it was no longer my worry. I did not say it out loud and nor did I seek a diagnosis, but there is a fair chance that due to excessive work I had suffered a physical breakdown. The term, the cause, the symptoms were not known to me, but I did know I was too young to feel such pressure and fatigue.

Six months and three days after I'd signed the sale contract, my childhood friend Nick (with whom I'd worked summers at the local SCUBA dive shop in Rockingham) called and asked if I could join a motor yacht in Monaco. The opening was that of a deckhand; he knew I held higher maritime qualifications, but it was a 'take it or leave it' offer. I said yes. I wanted a break from my surroundings, to make a bold change towards another path; something that seemed daring from a distance but had a safety net. I was still buying the outrageously priced yachting magazines and knew deep within me that all the recent turmoil was with purpose. I was soon to be a yacht crew.

This so far unrequited desire to join the community I had first seen during the 1987 America's Cup was my primary motivation, but possibly there was also some fear of where remaining in Australia might or might not take me. What if I could not chart a career that would be comparable with that of my friends, both in and out of the military? My fear was that if I competed on equal territory, my performance could be measured. I had accumulated success in the navy and then in business, but I never felt settled in either. I still needed to find 'that community' that I belonged to and that wanted to embrace me.

Additionally, to 'get out of town fast and join a yacht in Monaco' certainly appealed romantically. It was 6 September 2001 and my world – and everyone else's – was about to change.

See where 'yes' takes you

There are no single reasons for many of life's bigger decisions and to try to find a rationality is most often fruitless – but at risk of sounding like a greeting card or a meme, be bold, and follow your instincts.

In love and life, my richest experiences have come from going out on the edge of the wild grass, where you are frightened and are relying on your wits. Follow every path until its end or until there is a new one ready to take you further.

When faced with a choice between yes and no – say yes, hang on tight and see where the opportunity takes you.

Part 2

BEST OF THE BEST

Learning the 'why'

When I joined my first motor yacht, the internet was not ubiquitous. Email addresses were in use but did not travel well, the term 'social media' had yet to be coined... it was a different time. Due to the combination of these factors and the relative size of the industry being smaller, I just didn't know as much on that first day, flying into Nice airport, as a modern crew member does after a glance at a website or social media platform. I was met at the airport by my friend Nick. Our lives had been divergent for some years, yet there were strong childhood bonds: golden memories that shone through the darkness of time. Nick had filled out since his youth, but retained his broad grin and same goofy laugh (sorry, Nick). I knew to travel light and only had one bag, which was just as well as the French hire car (the unstoppable Renault Twingo) was a lot smaller than my Australian eyes were used to. We drove towards Monaco, my eyes swivelling constantly as I tried both to listen to Nick and take in all I was seeing. I remember thinking that the infrastructure along the coast was tired (it would only age further in subsequent decades) but being in awe of the tunnels into Monaco. Tunnels that have grown and multiplied many times since.

Monaco. What did I know about Monaco? Princess Grace, Formula 1 motor racing, Elvis and a childhood movie about a

Volkswagen Beetle called Herbie that had come to life. I wasn't even sure if the place was real or a Hollywood construct. My Australian education and life experience to that point was centred around South Asia, the Pacific and the UK. Europe was a single mass with a few country-specific clichés thrown in. It is embarrassing to say that in that Renault Twingo all those years ago, if I was handed a blank map of Europe and asked to fill in the spaces with country and city names, I would not have got very far. Luckily, there was no quiz, and as we left the tunnels I saw Port Hercule Monaco for the first time. Even with the glorious Sydney Harbour as my reference, I was completely overwhelmed by the scale of the yachts along the T-jetty and around the inner harbour, which has doubled since that time. The magazines had not prepared me for such a density of wealth in one location – it didn't make sense. How did this enclave exist and how could you fit so much into such a small space?

On that first day, I never expected that I would come to know this quirky little principality as intimately as my childhood home. I would learn all the public, but discreetly placed, 'ascenseurs' that lift and lower the pedestrians to save walking the myriad steps within this Escheresque community. I would learn where the small 'off-street' stores were that sold bargains, even in Monaco. I would knock on nondescript doors of apartments converted into private offices serving some of the most powerful families in Europe and the world.

I had also never seen a vessel 'Mediterranean moored' in the true sense. I knew from maritime college of the practice of setting anchors and backing into a port, but there had been no need for it in the southern hemisphere. It was wonderful to see hundreds of metres of jetties with yachts all tied up 'stern to'. I was in awe of the immense skill of the yacht captains with their vessels so carefully docked. Lost in my thoughts, I also realised that everywhere I looked there were crew busily working in their matching uniforms. I was returned to 1987, the America's Cup, and a dream that had taken so long to be realised. As I stepped on board this superyacht, my new workplace/ home, I tried to be nonchalant, but I couldn't help but be overwhelmed. Not only was the yacht itself beyond anything I could have comprehended, but I was also joining an industry that I had looked to longingly in the magazines for so long. Never would I have thought on that first day that within five and a half years I would be the captain of one the largest superyachts in the world.

Yes, I was self-conscious. After all, I was a small-town boy from 'anywhere' Australia and felt the crew of these yachts must be the elite of the maritime industry, the best of the best. Without even having met a crew member, I just knew they had to be better seafarers than me or anyone I had worked with. How could you not be, when you were given such an incredible workplace? It also dawned on me that until this moment I had been proud of my maritime career. I had received tertiary education at a naval academy, completed a gruelling navigation education and then sailed internationally. I had also skippered harbour craft, tugs and offshore support vessels in Northern Australia. In parallel, I was an accomplished ocean racer. All this narrative came crashing down around me when

I looked around the port from the side deck of the yacht. It was like being back on the tug for the first time. I knew nothing.

Prior to joining, there were no security checks, rounds of interviews or even a check of certification. It was a private yacht registered in St Vincent and the Grenadines and largely unregulated. This is not to say the yachts were not professional, but professionalism was voluntary. I could have been anyone, and nobody really cared. The yacht had been built by its former owner, the Mexican billionaire Emilio Azcárraga in 1991, and was outrageous. It had three waterjets as propulsion, a gas turbine for power, and sported three decks of outlandishly curved windows inspired by Parisian buses. None of this really entered my consciousness as I was just dealing with my own nerves. I spoke only English and the assumed worldliness of all the crew left me feeling small. I had heard of Antibes, Nice, Portofino, but where they were in real distances in relation to each other – no idea. The euro was new and the dual pricing was confusing; ATM machines were not globally linked and while I had some US dollars left over from time working in Hawaii, I was not completely sure how I would be able to get money.

These thoughts flooded my overwhelmed mind in the minute or so it took to walk from the transom to the bridge with Nick, who said he had just enough time to take me to the captain. Yes, I too had sailed as 'skipper' for commercial vessels, but the captain of this yacht was of an entirely different cut to me. He commanded this vision of beauty, and he was the one who had reversed her into Monaco's port, between two other yachts of comparable size, with only the smallest gap between their gleaming white hulls. The pneumatically sealed, hydraulically powered bridge doors cantilevered back and as I stepped across the threshold onto the darkened bridge, I felt my heart rate instinctively quicken with nerves. I could hear a South African accent; the captain was on the phone and I was interrupting. I wanted to be there but also wished I was back in Sydney. I stood sheepishly by the door as it closed behind me. Nick had to get on with his day, and he left me to it.

Barry White was playing louder than it needed to be for mid-morning and as I waited for the captain to finish his call, it was the strains of 'I'm Gonna Love You Just A Little More Baby' that kept me company. With some jet lag, I was losing myself to the music when the captain, André, finished his call and turned to me. 'You Aussies don't have a chance, the Boks have your number.' Our first greeting was a harbinger of many conversations that would follow, based around the long feud on the rugby field between our respective South African and Australian national teams. I loved rugby and was an avid follower of the Wallabies, the Australian national team, and until days previously had even been the neighbour of their fearless half back. I responded, 'You don't have a chance – the Boks can't pass and are playing yesterday's game.' I knew what I had said, but it wasn't my voice – how did my nerves do that to me? In the broadest Afrikaans accent, my new captain said, 'My boy, you Aussies are so full of shit. Let's get morning tea.' I was not to know it on this first day, but André's and my life would connect for the subsequent 20 years; we would come to know each other's families and homes with intimacy. To this day, whenever I hear Barry White, I think of André. Yes, it's awkward.

As my first captain, I will always have a respect for André, a man with looks that are somewhere between an evening newsreader and the mate you wished wasn't with you when you saw a pretty girl. In the early days of our shared time sailing together, I did not appreciate or understand the awareness André had to the 'why' of yachting. I had joined the yacht from a commercial environment that valued paperwork and process. André, who at that point was a mere 12 years into what would develop into a 30-year yachting career, dismissed my commercial distractions as he understood entirely the point of a superyacht. It's all about the guests. If it did not directly impact the guest experience, André was only tangentially interested. This needs to be read in the context where the Large Yacht Code, which details the safe operation of the yachts, had yet to be written, and safety was more about good judgement than a compliance obligation. Yes, the yacht conducted drills and I never felt that André did not take the crew's safety and his own responsibility seriously, but these drills were undertaken as something that needed to be done and not the focus, whereas my earlier experience had been the reverse. André recognised that the hotel services were the products of the yachting business. He made allowance, to my chagrin at the time, that disruptive or even lazy crew were to be embraced if they were recognised by the guests. Years passed and compliance and administration became much more a part of my life, but my recognition of the rationale of yachting came from those formative years with André. He never lost sight of the fact that yachting should be fun. For the guests and for the crew, his rules were few and he let the show go on around him.

I was issued with a uniform and a radio and put to work straight away. It was Friday and the boat was being washed down. I went outside after lunch to join the deck team; most were English and there was a healthy banter and good music on the deck speakers. Pretty quickly I realised that while they were friendly and welcoming, it was clear to all that I didn't know a thing. I didn't even know what the tools were, let alone what to do with them: what was a deck squeegee or a doodlebug? And most concerning, what was a Kiwi love glove?

The deck team was led by Steve, the recently promoted first officer. He was wary of me, not having the strongest relationship with my friend Nick, who as the chief engineer should not have been hiring deckhands. I realise now the limb Nick went out on for his childhood friend, and I remain grateful for this. Steve was professional in all aspects, and I recognised this quickly. He was immaculately presented, self-disciplined and demanding of his team. At the time, this made him somewhat of an outlier from the norm, and it would take years before others with Steve's commitment would begin to flow into the yachting industry.

My career as a naval officer, area manager for P&O Maritime and a high-performing, even if somewhat rogue, ship's agent meant I had always had responsibilities. While I was looking forward to the change, I didn't quite know how to respond when Steve said to me one day when I was inside the yacht, 'What are you doing here? Deckhands shouldn't be seen inside before the end of the day.' It was the reality and what I was looking for when I left Sydney, but I wasn't ready to not be 'managing' something. But after the first few days of not quite knowing what was going on, I settled into the yachtie routine. At the age of 30, I was an older deckhand and having had some playful years behind me I never felt the need to 'party like a yachtie'. Of course, in hindsight this may have been an opportunity missed, but with Steve and André as educators I was on my way in a new career. Given how much swagger I had recently presented on the safe home ground of Sydney, it was quite confronting and yet relaxing at the same time to be the 'new guy'. Very little was expected, which was just as well – I did not have much to offer.

Steve had ordered some new dock lines before the planned departure across the Atlantic. Dock lines are ropes in multiples of 100 metres in length and 24mm in diameter; they fill a car easily. A green Mercedes wagon with German registration plates stopped by the gangway and, on the radio, I was directed to meet the car and arrange for the lines to be brought on board. The agent was a German, Christiane, who was being assisted by another German-speaking woman, maybe a couple of years younger than I was. The two ladies moved around the dock and to the gangway as if they owned it, directing crew to meet their needs. The younger agent wore glasses and was striking in that her hair was cropped short, very short, similar to the style of the Eurythmics lead singer, Annie Lennox. It was some surprise the next day when the 'Annie Lennox' agent appeared in the crew mess and in a uniform. It seems André and Christiane had spoken and the vacancy the yacht had for a lead service (what was lead service again?) was to be filled by this young, attractive Austrian girl, Yvonne. Lead service, I would learn, is most closely aligned with a hotel restaurant manager, which is exactly what Yvonne had been in Austria and most recently also in Bermuda. With Steve's rebuke in mind, I kept clear of the interior of the yacht during working hours, but even from a distance and from glimpses during meals I could see that Yvonne was moving at twice the pace of the others in the interior and was beginning to 'shake the tree'. She had a competence that was absent in her department and a confidence in a new environment that I was lacking.

We left Monaco three days later, sailing west towards Gibraltar, and Yvonne was not on board. During a meandering afternoon watch on the bridge, André asked me about us hiring Yvonne full time, as the days in Monaco had only been a trial, and he was considering whether she should join us on the yacht's arrival in Fort Lauderdale. I am not sure if he was interested in my response as much as just passing time on the bridge, but as he asked the question I realised that while we had only spoken a few times, I missed the energy Yvonne brought with her and that I was missing her presence. She was more interesting than the others in the crew and I had thought it would be good to spend more time with her. But for the second time in our very short professional relationship, I responded daftly to André's question: 'She seems a bit too serious, but was professional.'

Really, is that the best I had? The bridge has a nice habit of allowing meaningless comments to float into the air and this was one that André chose to just let pass. Among many 'sliding door' moments that life presents, this conversation on a quiet afternoon at sea may have been one of my greatest.

If André had chosen to heed my comment on Yvonne being too serious and not offer her the permanent position, my life would read very differently. Yvonne did join us in Fort Lauderdale and in a very natural way we sought each other's company. We shared an interest in using the opportunities that a global cruising yacht presented to explore incredible destinations. We began to align our days off work to make trips away to Bermuda, Nuku Hiva, Tahiti, Panama, Galapagos and New Zealand. We hiked, scuba-dived, took scooters and rode bikes wherever we could. As weeks became months and months multiplied, our lives became inseparable.

Yvonne and I would sail together, fall in love, move ashore, move back to sea, marry and start a family, and 20 years on we continue our journey, side by side. We travelled continents, overcame obstacles and laughed and loved together. We are parents to two wonderful daughters and Yvonne is at the core of my being. Without her unwavering support, I would not have had the confidence to approach the challenges I have undertaken, for better or worse, through my captaincies.

It's not about the boat

It is easy to focus on the yachts themselves – they are wonderful – but in those early days and throughout my career, I never forgot that there was someone funding the adventure. There are no yachts, crew or industry without the yacht owners. I was never star-struck by the individuals, but the sheer size of the wealth was truly daunting. It was always in my thoughts that everything I was surrounded by had been purchased by the yacht owner. My toothbrush, my socks, my sun cream and the food I ate. If I let my mind wander across the breadth of the wealth, I would find myself lost. These yacht owners had benefited most greatly from humanity's ledger of rewards and opportunities.

Over the years I have fielded many questions from friends and casual acquaintances on the nature of the yacht owners. I deflect and demur mostly, but I think it fair that some myths are dispelled and others accepted as truths. I am annoyed by the portrayals, from the Michael Douglas character preaching 'Greed is Good' in *Wall Street* to the try-hards, such as the the gaudy influencer and reality television types, who will never be recognised in the group due to a lack of wealth, class and discretion. Having said that, not all the billionaires I have shared time with live up to my ideals, but perhaps those ideals are unfair. Even with the insights I have into their fallibility (as gruesome as my own), I nevertheless hope for more from these Copernican centres of the financial solar system. I want all the billionaires to have a little Gianni Agnelli style sprinkled with some Aristotle Onassis intrigue, topped off with some Paul Allen vision. Though today's billionaires are often in sneakers, hoodies and jeans, those that I have spent time with have given me insight into a world I could never have known existed during my sandy and sunburnt childhood, clinging to the edge of the Australian continent.

The modern billionaire yacht owner holds a wealth that is hard to understand. I have glanced at the Forbes List or other equivalent rich lists when caught by clickbait, and they give some titillation by showing one view of who really does sit at the top of the world's financial tree. There are familiar names and families, names from popular brands or media barons who are as often in the news as making it, and many names whose wealth is described in a minimalistic three lines by word-conscious editors. There is also another group, the billionaires whose wealth is not so easily found in the public domain. I now look to these lists with some scepticism, as from what I have seen... they're not even close. With the utmost respect to the various organisations that build the rich lists, their researchers, however diligent, can only use information that is in the public domain. Private or obscured holdings are not included. This is startling to me. The published wealth gap is already phenomenal, and the yacht owners I know well all have wealth that is multiples of what is published.

Planetary theory

I once described the yacht-owning billionaires in comparative terms to nation states, and in direct financial correlation by wealth this remains correct. Where my description was wrong was that a number-by-number correlation only tells part of the story. They are so much more. The world of the billionaire is so hard to describe; modern fiction cannot do it justice and factual accounts show only what is chosen to be shown. My comment to the Hollywood director being shown the yacht was spot on: nobody would believe it.

When Copernicus challenged a 1,000-year-old theory, it was disruptive, heretic and, as time would show, correct: 'We revolve around the Sun like any other planet.' The billionaires are the suns in their universe. Their solar system contains planets built of information and access. Like Copernicus's sun, they don't seek either: information and access are captured by a gravity that circles the billionaires. Those in the inner circle are the satellites to the information and access. When the billionaire directs their attention onto the satellite, it is the sun coming across the horizon; when they move on it is darkness, absolute darkness. I have been a satellite many times, and when that sun shines it is glorious; the billionaire's attention makes everything grow and warms the skin. When their attention is lost, it is cold, and it is always the billionaire who chooses the sunset. Billionaires rarely move without their solar system in place. As their focus shifts, so does the orbit of information and access. There are no bounds to this: world leaders, CEOs or local markets, they all feed them. They also leverage off each other: when giants stand on the shoulders of giants, their view extends past all visible horizons.

Similarly, a table showing where superyachts are built only tells half the story, and the same is true for the yacht owners. It does not address their intent for ownership, how they use their yacht or who accompanies them. None of these measures are reported because those reporting do not know. It is easy to say that 22 per cent of yachts are owned by US residents (this is about correct), but it is much harder to say definitively that 50 per cent of yachts are used to entertain the owners' families, 25 per cent are used as a way of minimising jurisdictional tax liabilities and 10 per cent are owned for the pure joy of the freedom they offer. You cannot generalise the behaviour of the billionaire yacht owners any more than you can make behavioural generalisations of any group, but due to the unique environment that they inhabit, they are the smallest and tightest cultural group in the world. The billionaire yacht owner 'normal' is so far removed from the 'normal' of the national or cultural community they notionally belong to that to find empathy they can only look to each other.

The self-made billionaires I spent time with all displayed a voracious appetite for knowledge, power, creation, relationships and wealth. Those who were born to families already with great wealth may not have this same innate hunger, but through their education and childhood experiences have acquired similar attributes. My observations dispute the well-trodden point of view that self-made wealth differs greatly to inherited wealth.

Does a Russian oligarch or Saudi prince have a lot in common with a Silicon Valley 'sandshoe billionaire'? Well, yes: there are established and finite ways to build private wealth structures, and this also shapes the behaviours of the billionaire yacht owners. Their travel plans will replicate each other (where they ski, sail and party), their children will attend a select group of schools and even their personal staff (like me) will move between the group. When billionaires meet, they will greet as old friends, even though they have likely never met before. A physical meeting is not needed for them to know each other's backgrounds; their respective lives are so well documented within their circle, even if shielded from the mainstream media, that histories are already known. They will behave with intimacy where there is none, they will speak of their children and of future collaboration. They will look to link their solar systems. It doesn't always work...

The yacht was anchored in St Barths for Easter. It was a family holiday for the yacht owner, but there was also a sailing regatta, 'the Bucket'. This humbly named event draws the best racers in the world, who leave their race-honed thoroughbreds for the more grandiose world of large sailing yachts. There is nothing like seeing thirty 50-metre-plus sailing yachts in open conflict on the water: the size, the loads, the cost, it is all staggering. The racers are warriors and give no compromise to the normally palatial sailing yachts they are racing. The winches scream under load, the lines sing, the yachts heel with aggression, and sometimes heavy loaded masts and spars 'let go' with the recoil of a Second World War battleship. Threading their way through these beautiful modern yachts are the glorious J-Class. The 'Js' are bedecked with America's Cup sailors, billionaires and those who are neither racers nor billionaires, but who do all the work so the former groups can revel in their own company.

I had brought the motor yacht to the regatta to allow the owner his time to race with the best in the world, among whom he made up for his every-so slight lack of skill with pure competitive determination. During the second day's sailing, a well-known interior designer contacted me. Could he bring a prospective billionaire client to tour the motor yacht? We both knew it was a big request: the yacht was an artistic wonder of design, but it was also a family home and needed to be respected as such. I told him I would ask the yacht owner, who returned, salt-encrusted, late in the afternoon. The J Class may have been conceived as a gentleman's yacht, but there were no gentlemen that day. The wind was heavy, the waves short and steep, and the yachts were under the waves as much as over them. My yacht owner was visibly tired and shaken. I should have noted this and said nothing, but I didn't and passed on the designer's request. The response was a vague 'Yes, OK, but please keep the tour away from the family'. As he was leaving, he said, 'Is this normal?' I told him it was to be taken as a compliment; the escorted guest was a yacht owner of significance and contemplating the purchase of another superyacht. His quizzical look, amplified by fatigue, should really have been a strong enough signal.

The guest arrived, flanked by two assistants (let's call them what they were: goons) who stayed on the swim platform as the designer, the guest, his partner and I toured. The designer and I narrated as we went around an 'approved' public route. The guest barely spoke or showed any acknowledgement of our presence throughout the tour. He spoke with his girlfriend in a muted tone, pointing and smiling towards some features, all the time taking no notice of my narrative. He asked politely, 'Can we see the master suite?' I apologised and pointed out it was a family home that was in use. My answer was not acknowledged but nor was it challenged. It was an uncomfortable hour, but the tour was finished, and the guests departed.

The next morning, the yacht owner called me to the breakfast table. He was rested and had thought through my request for the tour; he was not happy with me, as he felt pushed. Billionaires should never feel pushed. I took my admonishment with the good grace of knowing I had made a mistake – not a terrible one, but a clear lapse of protocol.

Two days passed and the tour was, I felt, a distant memory. I once again greeted the yacht owner on return from a gentler day's sailing. He called me to the side and asked if some measure of thanks had been received for the tour: a card, a bouquet, a reciprocal invitation he could decline. I shook my head to indicate I had not heard from the designer or the guests since the tour, knowing as I did that I should have prompted the other yacht's captain to organise the thank-you gift. My yacht owner glanced to the horizon and said, 'Never again. Never ask me for permission for a tour for someone I do not know.' 'Yes, I understand,' I replied.

What the fellow billionaire, of recent wealth, did not appreciate is that there is a firm code of conduct. Thank-you notes are important; visits have a protocol matching those of heads of state and they cannot be ignored. Billionaires circle each other with care.

Be courteous like a billionaire

In an endless search for efficiency and a more egalitarian society, we have dispensed with protocols of civility. In the digital pace of the modern world, thank-you cards, dress codes for meals and overt courtesy may seem to be from a time long past.

I say: bring them back. Slow it down, take care and look for others to do the same. The billionaires retain these for a reason: they make each event that little bit more memorable – special.

Wind of change

I have drifted away, my attention indulgently focusing on the intrigue of the yacht-owning billionaires. My time on deck was foundational for my career but I had not joined the superyacht community to stay a deckhand. I aspired to captaincy, and I applied myself towards this goal. The cultural and technical skills that were specific to superyachts made for a steep learning curve, yet it was not long until the knowledge from the navy, commercial maritime and businesses ashore began to provide me with an advantage. Yacht careers are more than varnishing and boat-washing. I held computer skills, understood accounts, navigation and the global maritime legal framework, and I could draw upon all this to make myself more valuable to the captains I served. I also read in the evenings everything I could find on the yachting industry and made an effort to help any trade contractor that came to the yacht. My (not so well hidden) agenda was to gain any insight they might have from their perspective. I was mindful that while I could only gain direct knowledge from the yachts I worked on, the contractors and industry professionals were visiting multiple yachts every week.

My simple approach of hard work, inquisitiveness and seizing opportunity allowed me to move through the developmental roles of bosun and second officer relatively quickly. As a chief officer I paused, as I felt that this was where I had greatest exposure to the knowledge I needed before taking the final and large leap to superyacht captaincy. That leap was seemingly visible, as I was about to receive my first offer of captaincy.

It was 2004 and I had departed from my new home in Austria thinking I was to join a newly purchased yacht as captain: my first yacht captaincy. Mid-flight across the Atlantic something changed, and the yacht's owners chose a captain they knew from a previous yacht. It would be a poor duty to the truth to say I was not disappointed and that I did not huff and puff for a few days. I called Yvonne several times and through her calming counsel and blind cheerleading I placed my ego to the side and went to work as the chief officer.

The chief officer is second to the captain when looked at in a straight command line, but it is a long way from captaincy. I was to lead the deck team and largely organise the day-to-day operations of the yacht, often a thankless job with the other departments resenting being told what to do by an 'equal'. It is also a time when an ambitious chief officer begins to 'practise' behaviours for when their time comes in the big captain's chair. I would like to say that, despite the last-minute change in job title, I kept my eagerness towards captaincy in check; my colleagues might not be so charitable in their reminiscences.

Drawing upon childhood and naval training, I have an innate respect for those I report to, and I supported the captain in his new role. It was his good fortune to have secured the role due to a historic relationship with the owners and I held no animosity towards him for my being on the wrong side of this. Where I did begin to feel some acrimony was when my new captain did not seem to relish the role the way I knew I would. In saying this, I need to break apart 'relish': he certainly relished the salary and the perks (as the deck team learned when they were cleaning his car). What he did not relish was the work needed in leading a team and keeping a complex yacht operating efficiently. The captain's cabin door was closed more than it was open, and the cabin empty as much as it was occupied. Due to the limited numbers on smaller yachts, I was also looking after the technology on board and saw all the crew's internet browsing history as it passed the firewall. My dear captain spent many hours a day watching UK football and when he was not viewing the games, he was looking to purchase a Louis Vuitton bag for his wife – hopefully his wife. The Mediterranean summer season was soon to begin and my 'spidey-sense' was telling me this captain was not taking it too seriously. I might need to cover some of the spaces he would leave blank.

The first few weeks of summer passed uneventfully, and maybe my checking of the browsing history did show some envy that I was trying to deny… The captain was certainly not doing more than he needed to do, but we were getting through the days and the new yacht owners warmed to his familiar face. The yacht owners were incredibly relaxed, and they showed respect to the crew. Their routines were predictable and their expectations consistent. I was not the captain, as I had hoped when boarding four months earlier, but I was still learning, and the days were passing easily.

The island of Mykonos, when viewed alongside Santorini, epitomises the Greek island ideal. Whitewashed villas, cobbled streets, bougainvillea growing across laneways and the ubiquitous turquoise waters. The pictures do not show that it is windy – really windy, dangerously and consistently windy. The meltemi wind blows from the north and is a major weather event, which joins hands with other global named events such as the Indian monsoon and the Azores High. We anchored on a glass-calm morning in front of the old town of Mykonos. It is a lovely sight, with the historic town to the east and the iconic windmills to the south. The town is seated within a bay that is open to the north and west; we were the only large yacht anchored in the area and had secured a prime location for the guests' breakfast. There is a morning routine on all yachts and in its simplest form it involves rinsing, washing and wiping. The full team were on deck to get everything in order before the guests arose. I was on deck by 5 am to co-ordinate the preparations, and noticed the dew that had formed on every exposed surface. It is not a scientific fact by any means, but dew often correlates to wind later in the day, the link being that there is a temperature difference somewhere that needs to be balanced.

I did not give the dew a second thought, as we were busy. New guests were arriving the next day and we had rubbish to take ashore, food to be brought on board and the family to entertain. The goal in yachting is to make the logistics invisible: guests know food must come from somewhere and cleaning happens, but they shouldn't see it. When this is woven in, a simple day becomes a complex start-stop game based on the guests' programme.

The yacht-owning family wanted to go ashore at four in the afternoon for a late lunch and a sunset stroll. A good plan, but the glass calm of the morning had given way to a solid 20 knots of wind by lunchtime. This concerned me, and I suggested to the captain during crew lunch that we should move around to the south of Mykonos ahead of the family's trip ashore. I followed up by stating the obvious: the yacht needed to be protected when the wind increased. My choice of speaking up in the crew mess may not have helped as the captain took my suggestion as a challenge to his competence. He doubled down, making sure all heard his rebuke to me as he affirmed his greater knowledge of the area. We would stay where we were.

I returned to deck and watched as the tenders bounced angrily around at the stern of the yacht. When the wind increases, a yacht at anchor will begin to yaw, swinging back and forth and bucking against her anchor chain. It is one of the most unpleasant feelings: uncomfortable for the guests, and each pull on the anchor could be the one that pulls it away from the seabed. In future years, in my own captaincy, I would pride myself on techniques to reduce yawing to virtually nil, but I was not the captain and we were yawing 50 degrees in either direction and the wind-driven waves were building.

At 3.45pm, I was waiting with the tender crew. We were joined by three additional crew who I had arranged to have standing by to assist with safe boarding. Promptly at four the family arrived, and I helped the parents and two teenage children to make the step into the tender, which was jumping behind the yacht like an excited puppy. As soon as they were seated, the deck crew swiftly let the lines go so the tender could move freely and not fight the lines of the yacht. Madame was decidedly uncomfortable, but her favourite deck crew, Eve, was in the tender with her and I could see her smiling once settled and being fussed over.

My saying 'Cup of tea?' was the signal to my team that we could all leave the stern of the yacht. There had been tension keeping the boarding safe, and there is nothing better than a shared tea to release it. I thought I would use the opportunity, in private this time, to talk with the captain about moving to the sheltered side of the island. The timing was on our side, the wind was still manageable, we had the benefit of daylight, and the family were away. A message to their driver ashore would bring them to a different destination without any disruption, and seeing Madame's face on departure I was sure it would be appreciated. We climbed the steps from the platform talking of who might do what during a move. There were tenders to be driven, cushions to be covered, water sports to be packed away: it was a lot of work.

I was third in the group alighting the steps when I saw the captain, chief engineer, second engineer and chief steward all walking towards us. There was a slight double-take from the deck team: we were all perspiring and wet with salt from the waves crashing across the swim platform, whereas the others were out of uniform. It didn't fit. During the summer season, months pass without seeing any crew out of uniform, and it was the visual impact more than any judgement of purpose that the 'shore clothes' represented. With the wind whistling across the aft deck, I could not hear what was said first but I heard the deckhand in front of me exclaim 'Are you serious?' and saw him shake his head with disrespectful disdain. I reached the top of the steps and the captain said at me, but not to me, 'When the tender comes back from this drop-off we are going to go ashore. We will come back just before the family.'

This was a point where I could have confronted the captain with this poor judgement: we had rising seas, strong winds and a tired crew. But I knew it would not have changed the outcome, and would only have brought animosity into the team. There was no way this gang of four would have turned around, changed back into uniform and returned to work because I thought it was windy. I said, 'Sure, the tender will be back in five minutes and the deck crew will look after you.' To the deck crew I said I was heading inside to make the tea. As I walked away, I saw in these four seniors the example of what I did not wish to be, an entitled and lazy leader.

In the time it took for the tender to return from the port after its second trip and for the deck team to regather for afternoon tea, the wind had increased further and the waves running down the side of the boat had risen to above a metre.

I relieved the second officer on the bridge for a while and sat there alone with my anxiety as the wind whipped the yacht from side to side and the tenders continued a perilous dance at the stern of the yacht. I knew what we needed to do, but I was not the captain and I could not unilaterally decide to relocate the yacht. To assuage my need to do something, I sent the captain a message via his phone: short and factual, stating my concern about the increasing winds. It was now five in the afternoon and there would have been just enough time to get around to the south and be anchored in time for the family.

His response astonished me. With no acknowledgement of my message, he ordered another tender be sent for more crew to join him. The chief engineer had been in touch with crew on board by phone and directed them to join. I used the radio to ask for a crew tender to be readied for a trip ashore. In the relaxed banter of the deck channel on the radio, I received 'Are you taking the piss?' as the response. I sought to de-escalate any tensions by saying only 'Please take care and be careful in the conditions'. I looked to the aft deck camera and saw four stewardesses skipping towards the stern of the yacht in the smallest of dresses. I held no malice towards them; they had been told by the chief engineer to come ashore to join the captain and they held no responsibility for weather-based safety decisions. The bridge internal phone rang, and it was the bosun: he asked in a halting voice whether he and one of the deck crew could go ashore too, as both their girlfriends were in the group and they wanted to join them. It didn't need to be said, but I knew the concern:

the senior crew ashore were known for lecherous behaviour and the deck crew wanted to be with their partners. Against all my better judgement, I said yes, so long as they could be back in time for the family's return.

For the next three hours I squirmed around the bridge, wondering how this situation would play out. It was now just past eight, darkness had fallen, the wind remained above 20 knots and the seas had risen to 1.5 and occasionally 2 metres. The yacht had developed a roll to the point of it being uncomfortable on board. Both tenders were now waiting in the port and neither the crew nor the family had been sighted. I handed the bridge back to the second officer so I could make my way to the stern of the yacht. It was intolerable just waiting with no control and no communications. I had sent several phone messages, but none had been answered.

It was 8.15pm and I was alone on the aft deck when the deck radio crackled on my hip. It was the tender driver telling the bridge he had all the crew that had been ashore on board his boat and they were moving slowly out of the port. Each time he pressed the radio to speak, I could hear the yelps of his passengers. I heard the second officer ask from the bridge how many there were on the tender. Between the squeals of the stewardesses in the background and the noise of the tender crashing through the waves at the port entrance, I heard the driver confirm he had all crew on board. The second officer challenged the driver across the radio that he was overloaded, and to make sure all had lifejackets on. The driver said he knew that he was overloaded but the captain wanted to bring all crew back together in the single tender, and all had lifejackets on.

I did not have enough crew remaining on board to safely bring this and the next tender to the yacht in these conditions if they returned close together. With both boats away and two of the strongest deck team ashore with the crew drinking group, it was me and one other. I could not ask the second officer to leave the bridge, so I asked for the chef and the night watch to be woken. It is very unfair to wake the night watch, but I had little choice. The chef and night watch stood with me as we saw the little tender smashing into the waves. It was clearly overloaded. Just as I was thinking how well the driver was adjusting to the conditions, one of the stewardesses leaned out over the side to be ill. Marvellous. The radio again came to life as the second tender confirmed they too were about to leave the port. They had put the folding weather cover up to protect the family and would make a slow path to the yacht. The bridge answered, confirming to them that the conditions at the stern of the yacht were uncomfortable and to ask Madame to remove her heels for safety. I made a mental note to compliment the second officer later on his presence of mind to suggest this.

The crew tender pulled up in a hail of screams. The driver was noticeably under pressure from the captain to get alongside fast. The unsteady crew on board the tender were struggling to throw the lines to allow us to tie them up. On the driver's third attempt we succeeded in securing them close to the ladder, and as I glanced up I could see that the guest tender was within 100 metres. All the crew in the first tender were soaked and I was embarrassed for them, but particularly the stewardesses, whose light cotton half-dresses were now completely transparent. The girls were being mocked and ogled in equal parts by the drunken senior male crew and it made me fume. In a tone I tried to make gentle and without admonishment, I told the girls to get straight inside, shower and change into uniform so as to be ready for the family. Their glassy-eyed stares in response made me rethink and I said they should go to their cabins and stay there unless called for.

As I looked to the bosun and the one deck crew, I saw the same eyes as the stewardesses: both were apologetic, saying they were 'forced' to drink ouzo shots by their seniors. I took this as a 50 per cent truth and said all was fine, but they needed to stay out of sight tonight; alcohol and rough weather are a potent mix. The last four crew on board were the first four that had departed. Led by the captain, they stepped back on the yacht, and I let them pass my turned shoulder unacknowledged. The family were on close approach and I instructed the first tender's lines to be thrown so the driver could stand off: we had no time and no crew to tie this boat up on the side of the hull, where it was too rough anyway. The four seniors were milling about on the swim platform, and in a firm but (I hoped) neutral tone, I said they had to leave as it was unsafe with the next tender coming. The engineers and the chief steward were already moving away, keen to get out of sight, while the captain lingered. 'Seriously, get the fuck away!' was the best I could muster. I think my tone no longer mattered.

The family were 5 metres from the yacht and huddled under the weather shield. In a guest tender we always had three crew; this made the passing of lines quicker than for the crew tender, and we had them alongside immediately. I could hear the yacht owner instructing his children, 'Go now and don't let go of the tender until you take Brendan's hand on the yacht.' He was an excellent yacht owner and parent in equal measure. He then instructed the tender driver to help his wife to the ladder, and with wide eyes she also took my hand as she stepped to the more stable yacht: she was clearly shaken. Only when he saw his family all safe did the owner make his way cautiously to the stairs, reaching forward and gripping my arm in a firm overhand fireman's grip, with me returning the hold by gripping his forearm. He was a smaller man and my hand completely encased his forearm. It felt awkward, as though I would crush his arm like an Easter egg.

Once all the family were on board, I gave a nod to the tender and as the two additional crew stepped out, the lines were thrown back and the tender, now with only the driver on board, joined the first and both sat in the wind shadow behind the yacht. It was not ideal; the wind was still building and in the darkness the waves were pounding the yacht as we aggressively pulled on the extremities of the anchor chain. I walked three paces behind the owner, ascending the stairs to the aft deck, and as my eyeline rose to the level of the deck I could see the swaying, soaked captain in a poorly cut shirt and cargo shorts, waiting to speak with the owner. I was appalled to be in the scene and wished I was anywhere else.

The captain said something that was hard to make sense of and the owner, with no acknowledgement of having heard, turned to me and asked what we should do. I said (in what may have been faux earnest tones), 'So long as the captain agrees, we should relocate to the south to seek shelter for the night.' The owner was experienced in the Mediterranean and asked me if I meant near the beach clubs. I confirmed that was correct and in a rhetorical tone he asked, 'Shouldn't we have moved earlier?' The question was an answer in itself.

It was too rough to lift the tenders out of the water. I told the two drivers they needed to follow for the one-hour relocation. It was not ideal, and I knew it: all deck crew had been working without a break for over 15 hours in the heat and wind. I sent two crew to prepare the anchor and I went to the bridge to make the move. To my astonishment, the captain was there when I arrived, in uniform now but still dishevelled and clearly drunk. He stepped forward to speak and I cut him off by telling him that if he said one word on the bridge that compromised safety, I would have him removed and it would leave me with no alternative but to report the entire afternoon's drunken debacle to the yacht owner. The bridge is always darkened for night navigation, and I hadn't noticed that the owner, who rarely came to the bridge, was sitting on the couch in the corner. He said nothing. The captain withdrew to the shadows and I did not give his presence another thought.

I had not manoeuvred the yacht since joining – the captain did not wish to share the bridge, lest it weakened his position. It was not the handling of the yacht that was a concern for me, it was that I did not know where the buttons were to activate the control levers that I needed to operate the engines and rudders. It took a couple of anxious minutes to piece it all together and the silence was broken only once by the owner asking in a very supportive voice if I was comfortable making the move in these conditions and in darkness. I thanked him for his concern and affirmed I was confident we could make the move safely, and the yacht would be in far better conditions in the new anchorage.

We picked up the anchor and turned to the west across the northerly waves. The yacht lurched through the turn and while I had no specific worry on safety, my thoughts turned to the service staff, who should have been walking through the interior checking nothing had fallen over and broken, but instead were lying in their beds, likely with buckets beside them. We moved through the turn quickly and with the sea and wind behind us the yacht steadied as we motored downwind, parallel to Mykonos. The stern was still being lifted by the waves and the bow would surf a little as the yacht accelerated, but the rolling from the turn was finished and the noise of the wind greatly reduced. Madame could now find some peace in her cabin.

There was one last problem: during the anchor recovery I had been looking directly at the lights of Mykonos town ashore. Those lights were now behind the yacht, and I was staring into an inky darkness. It was a moonless night and I could not see anything. Night vision, where your eyes move from cone to rod vision, is critical to mariners and takes about 30 minutes to transition. I had no time to wait for this and peering through binoculars to make out the south-west corner of Mykonos or the small island of Krommidi further south was a pantomime I was playing for the sake of those watching. We were safe, and I had the radar and the electronic charts to confirm this to me, but still it would have been nice to have seen something, anything, in confirmation.

There was a movement at the back of the bridge, and as I turned away from the navigation screens I saw that it was the owner getting up off the couch. I shared, without his asking, that the yacht would be on this heading for 45 minutes before turning to the shelter of the southern bay and the new anchorage. I also confirmed we would be fully anchored within one and a half hours. He was backlit by the now distant glow of Mykonos town but I could see him nod in understanding. The owner moved to depart the bridge, paused, and asked if the crew in the tenders were OK. It was kind of him to ask, and I said they were fine following the yacht and we had radio communications with them. Again, he nodded in acknowledgement, with one hand now on the door leading from the bridge to his suite.

We anchored, the tenders rejoined, and we were sheltered. I, along with all the deck team, had worked a 19-hour day and we sought the comfort of a few hours' sleep before starting the morning routine again. The next morning arrived all too quickly, and nobody said a word about the previous day. Late morning, after not seeing the captain anywhere, I slipped an envelope with a courteous resignation under the closed door. It pushed aside two other envelopes that had been placed ahead of it. The day before seemed to have incited more action than conversation.

To emulate or not to emulate?

I had now identified the captain I did not wish to be, and it was time for me to work out exactly what captain I could be. I have been blessed with positive role models, but I think I have learned more from those I do not wish to emulate.

I have rarely reached the standards I seek for my own performance, but knowing where I did not want to take my leadership provided a reference to behaviours I would not succumb to.

Master under God

The path to superyacht captaincy is not an easy one. The market is small and cloistered, with captains' roles often being chosen on the basis of friendship or loyalty as much as competence. I knew, having just missed a chance that had been set in place for me, that I would have to invest more time to be recognised as ready. I did not leave the yacht immediately after that awful day in Mykonos. It is expected that no matter what happens, the season will be finished, and the loyalty to your mates, instilled if not beaten into me as a navy cadet, remained, so I sailed with the team until the autumn.

I did use the rundown time to ruminate a little on what and where I was heading. Yvonne and I were soon to marry, and it seemed the right moment to question everything. Should I stay at sea once married? And if yes, should it be in this freewheeling world of yachting? Seafaring is an interesting choice of lifestyle that is not for everyone, and in my own experiences I have been both enamoured and disenchanted with a life at sea, at times oscillating between the two views in the space of hours. I have always loved being on the water, but after three weeks of seeing nothing but the ocean and the same few crew, the difference between concept and reality sinks in. I had worked in shore offices and always felt displaced, so I knew there wasn't an office waiting for me somewhere.

Aside from acknowledging the life of the seafarer, there was also the question of captaincy. Times had moved forward, but I recalled from my studies the phrase used in Victorian England for sea captains signing on: 'Captain xxxx is Master under God for this voyage on the Ship xxx.' The phrase might have been a century out of use, but still, once clear of the shore, the captain's ultimate responsibility remained unrefuted. Did I even want this? The navy and commercial vessels were an incredible introduction to life at sea and gave a unique opportunity to observe their own versions of captaincy, but both were very structured operating environments. And I mean *structured*: there is a navy reference book, with pictures, to show how a beard and sideburns should look. I think the sideburns were to be not more than 2cm wide. It was not until I discovered superyachts that I realised the challenge of leading with freedom. I had grown a little more comfortable with having space in the workplace since my agency experiences, but I still looked to see where the lines were on the playing field.

Superyacht captaincy, with its almost boundless opportunities to create a team culture within an unbelievable environment, seems an intoxicating mix. It was only as I learned the impact of these freedoms from watching others, such as my captain in Mykonos, that I realised it actually placed another layer of weight in leading a team. A weight that I would feel every day and always question if I was truly capable of carrying. I would seek in the future to lead and motivate a crew, protect the marine environment, uphold the laws applicable to the yacht and maintain the value of the asset. Somewhere among all this I was also expected to deliver an unparalleled guest experience to the most discerning guests in the world. Could I do all these things? I looked to those ahead of me on this journey for their special something that seemed to make it all fit together.

A superyacht is an embodiment of a complex system where the inputs do not guarantee the outcome. Somewhere there is a secret sauce that makes a yacht go from good to great and often this sits with the captain. I looked to others who did not seem to be as burdened as I was with this constant internal dialogue about performance expectations: was there a golden thread in their behaviours I could find? There were captains bordering on flippant about their roles – maybe they had it right and I was overthinking? Why couldn't I just enjoy it, claim a great lifestyle and what will be will be? At times I wish this could have been my way too, but it wasn't. I did care, I did want to do my best and while I never placed an unrealistic expectation to be the 'best superyacht captain', I did expect to be the best I could be. This internal challenge/tension was a fantastic motivator. I wanted to step out there, to get as close as possible to my own limits, fail if that's what was needed to find out where my edge was going to be. I often try to express myself in sports metaphors when lacking the ability to describe something well. My 'infinite squash court' theory remains one of my favourites.

Tennis or squash?

Leadership ashore is like tennis. It's tough, sure, but there is time to change ends, have a drink and think between games.

Leadership at sea is more like squash, with a ball that never stops bouncing, with an opponent that never misses a return. Every time you hit the ball it comes back faster and doesn't stop.

And this is what makes it so wonderful.

Run, Forrest, run

A superyacht operates globally and adheres to tight compliance obligations, with no compromise allowed for standards of performance. The billionaire yacht owners of my experience have an expectation that is without comparison – at risk of labouring this point, I really mean without reference anywhere. There is very little – well, no – understanding of second-rate performance.

I was still overthinking and after a little time looking to the job market, I found I was not quite competitive. Maybe the hesitation I felt was externally apparent, or more likely I was just not as strong as the others presenting for the same roles. Whatever the truth, I spent longer working on deck and sailing as a chief officer than my qualifications required. I knew I did not want a repeat of those first days in Darwin where I was long on ideas and short on knowledge, so I invested time to cover the gap. I wanted to be a successful superyacht captain and did not want to rush the process, so I rejoined André as relief captain: yes, we found each other again.

Over the next 12 months, André gave me the scope to really learn what yacht captaincy meant, and while I was progressing well from his tutelage I still wasn't ready for what happened next. In 2006 there was a shortage of commercially qualified Master Unlimited mariners with a strong yachting pedigree. Looking back, even by this definition, I was thin on experience to be approached, but I worked hard, learned fast, and when necessary I talked a good talk. The wonderfully caring founder of one of the leading crew placement agencies rang with a potential captain's position. 'They're looking for someone just like you and there is nobody else,' he said.

The call was a boost for my confidence, but I didn't think I would be competitive for the role, nor the yacht that the crew agent described – at that time, one of the largest in the world. However, I wanted at least the chance to be interviewed, and I thought about what I might be asked. Technical questions to define my experience – what was my awareness of maritime law and compliance? Where had I cruised? What ports did I know? What were the biggest seas I had encountered? There had to be a focus on what exposure I'd had to delivering guest experiences, with what cultures, and how innovative I was in creating unique itineraries. I had prepared truthful, yet stock, answers for each of these questions that would hopefully represent me as the glorious Master and Commander, a cross between the Patrick O'Brian character made famous by that other dashing Australian seafarer, Russell Crowe, and a Marvel character. I needed to make the interviewer aware that captaincy was a position for which I had all the training – training that had been tested by experience – and, ultimately, that this was a role I was born for.

At the same time, I wondered if it was just about being in the right place at the right time. I held the qualification needed for the role and my background matched in some way what was being sought. The match being someone else's judgement, someone who did not know me, nor (in any intimacy) the role I was being proposed for. I was beset by imposter syndrome before the interview process even began.

What would actually happen was that when the captain's cabin door was closed – long after this first interview, extending to years and multiple captaincies – I would continue to question if I really had what it took to deliver what was being asked. As my competence and confidence broadened, this decreased, and I reflect now that if I did not feel uncertain and unworthy in those early days, it would only have meant that I did not fully understand the huge demands of the role.

I was not the ideal candidate, but the crew agent's brief played on my mind: 'there is nobody else.' After several phone interviews, my recruitment moved forward to a face-to-face interview. It would be over dinner as the interviewing senior captain, Glenn, had split his flight routing to meet me. It was a warm Georgia evening when I met Glenn at Savannah/Hilton Head airport, and we exchanged brief pleasantries during the drive. I chose a street-side café in Oglethorpe Square, a relaxed yet nice restaurant in sight of the bench where Tom Hanks sat in *Forrest Gump*. Glenn was not overly impressed with the Gump reference – I would learn over time his clear preference for British over US culture.

Glenn was at that time the captain of one of the biggest and easily the most complex yacht in the world. He was as quick-witted as any person I had met, and spoke in a staccato flow, lingering over phrases and weighting words to make a point or for comedic value. We had been together for well over an hour before any talk of the yacht or employment began. I learned that Glenn had received a hefty speeding ticket in Germany, that he was stopping through to see me as a detour on the way to Vancouver where he would be inspecting the construction progress of a private submarine, and that he had just bought a Labrador pup for the family. The Labrador received the longest review, with Glenn recounting how he rebutted the request from his children for the dog to live inside during winter due to the cold, his response: 'They are called Labradors for a reason, it's fucking cold there.' Glenn had a confident, raucous and infectious laugh and for an hour I just laughed along to a series of great stories and impersonations, all delivered with professional poise.

I would learn over time that this was Glenn's default setting. He would cover his great intellect with seemingly banal anecdotes to lull the listener into thinking there was no substance to his banter. When Glenn sensed that point had been reached, he came in fast and hard with facts drawn from a near bottomless memory. If this seems like a plan, it wasn't – it was just Glenn's way of enjoying a conversation.

Some do not see the subtlety and feel as though they are the mouse to Glenn's verbal cat, playing until he chooses to finish the game. In Savannah I was not the mouse, but certainly I was receiving more than I was contributing. Rightly so too: Glenn was already an incredibly accomplished captain, flying around the globe to support the greatest yacht schedule in the world. He dressed well and oozed confidence; I dressed poorly and was nervous, conscious of my hands stained by paint, my shoes matching my hands and the next task on my current to-do list being to varnish a wooden rail in a shipyard. Somehow, among all this, I was offered the position to be his co-captain, which of course I accepted. Superyachts operate 365 days a year and require two captains to maintain this, the normal rotation being three months' working and three months' leave. In reviewing my motivation for accepting this role (which was above my demonstrated competence at the time), I see that the only thing stronger than my self-doubt was my attraction to finding the edge to my performance. In reviewing how I was ever offered this role, I returned to the recruitment agent's comment: 'there is nobody else.'

On first joining the great yacht, I am not even sure I was daunted. I was so far out of my depth that I could not touch the sides. I joined and just picked things up, hoping to do so before those around me – the crew, the family, office shore staff and ultimately the guests – could notice my lack of knowledge. I was straight back to that feeling I had standing in the wheel house of the tug, some ten years earlier, not knowing what would happen next. I was insatiable in my efforts to learn the yacht and its people, and focused on just avoiding catastrophe until Glenn, now my co-captain, returned from his leave, but would it be enough? Sadly, yachting and the maritime world does not work this way. There can be no 'just holding it together'. During my tenure there were medical emergencies, an equipment failure that almost sank the yacht, and the more mundane but nevertheless critical events that pepper a captain's day.

Learn fast, work harder

Emergencies do not know who is in charge – or, more correctly, they tend to find holes in the competence of those trying to keep them from the room. You cannot hope someone else's competence will fill the gap.

There is no other path than to learn faster and work harder if you want to extend yourself beyond your previous performance.

Advancing my journey

The crew were quite different to those from my previous yachting experiences. Firstly, there were a lot of them. There were 65 on board, with almost 100 on the payroll. I was not daunted by the numbers and drew upon the example and creed of my naval captains: learn your people.

I would learn home towns, children, sports and whatever I could to assist my leadership. The team were dominated by commercial cruise ship experience; these big companies provide excellent maritime training and experience but are a completely different culture to yachting. There was a clique that did not want to adapt to the 'yachtie ways' and I did hear condescension towards my recent yachting-dominated history, even though that experience was one of the reasons I had been chosen for the role. One of the chief engineers, who had both passenger and cargo experience, was quite dismissive of my message to the department heads that I was here to develop the culture to one that was 'guest experience first'. This was the mandate I had been given at my engagement, and regardless of my lack of confidence it was the one component of the role that I had to forge ahead with. I was still horribly self-aware as regards my knowledge of this incredibly complex yacht, but as I settled I began to realise why I was chosen. I knew how to relate to people, and I knew from previous yachts what guests are expecting. Yes, I was the right person to shift the culture.

The chief engineer and I bumped along for a while and only after a significant and critical event did he realise that there was a lot we could both offer and that our two backgrounds were not in conflict but complementary. Always prudent with words, the taciturn engineer said in his strong Yorkshire accent, 'You're not the cornflake-box captain I had you for.' I thanked him and walked away, wondering if that really was a compliment. The term 'cornflake box' is derogatory, implying that a qualification is as worthless as a trinket from a cereal packet. Before the incident, that is who I was to him; even now, I still had a long way to go.

Nevertheless, I was the 'right guy at the right time' for the role as defined by the yacht's owners and their representatives, and I did help adjust the focus of the yacht away from an operations-centric, commercial culture to a more guest-orientated approach. The yacht became more creative and, rather than relying on the equipment, the crew became more the centre of the show. The guests joined the crew for treasure hunts, games nights, concert evenings, sports events and an over-the-top, way too scary for teenage children, possibly psychologically scarring Halloween evening. Yes, it was I who suggested the great idea of lifting a crew member from the water with a crane, seemingly coming from nowhere (he had a concealed scuba cylinder to allow his extended time underwater) and have him bite down on a fake blood capsule as he left the water. I just did not expect Chad, the crew member, to look so dead when he came out. I really did think I had messed up terribly as the children screamed and ran away, and I was left facing their parents and all the guests with their hands across their faces in horror (think Edvard Munch's *The Scream*).

Halloween maybe held aside, I look back with pride that I made a contribution. Parallel to this is the awareness that I was in no way experienced enough for the role and while I thought, as with the tug, that this was my secret, it was on show to all in the early days. But as with the tug, hard work and application to learning helped me achieve the performance I wanted, and that which others relied upon.

Through this and my next roles I was well advanced on my journey towards developing professional competence, but not far enough. I think I was some way into my fourth significant captaincy when I started to realise just how much of what I did daily I did not know before. It sent a shudder through me: how had I even snuck through without disaster? I realised that although I couldn't skip steps on this path, I did not have to go it alone. I was already drawing upon the skills of the crew around me and in addition I sought mentors and peers to support and coach me. This was not usual at the time among superyacht captains: there was a cultural expectation that you should have all the answers alone and to demonstrate that you did not expose your vulnerability. I knew it might have made me an outlier, but I regarded my seeking support and counsel as providing me with a position of strength and not weakness.

Outcome over ego

I never needed/wanted to be the centre of the picture, but I felt others had this expectation. They didn't. I took a leap forward when I realised people were not watching me: they were watching the outcome.

Most simply wanted their problem solved, and passed no judgement when I said I needed to speak to others, to a mentor, to my co-captain.

Will it be rough tonight?

Surfers live by the weather and I grew up with this obsession. My childhood home in Rockingham was only a bicycle ride from many surf spots that were humble, but more than enough for a boy. The moisture on the grass in the morning, the movement of the trees, the clouds: they were all indicators that I looked to daily. From my school classroom I could see if there was a swell on the horizon and I would gaze absently, longingly at the long lines moving towards the Western Australian coast, Rottnest Island catching the best of them. I was a good student and mostly escaped rebuke for this, but I did catch one comment from an earnest geography teacher who chastised me with 'You will never get anywhere staring out the window to the sea'.

I have made a career from staring out of many windows to the sea and if I were to teach, I would not hinder any student from gazing at the movements of the oceans and the skies. Staring towards the horizon during school was only part of the story. I would watch the Australian national news of an evening to see if there was a low making its way across the Southern Ocean to Western Australia, and by age 16 I believed I could feel it in the air if there was a swell coming to the islands that fringed the coast. Whether my belief was correct or not, we would nevertheless head out in small boats, chasing surf, as soon as the school week was finished. Studying meteorology was compulsory at the naval college; I learned the structure behind what I had felt, and something that would become a lifelong fascination, bordering on addiction, began.

What is the worst weather you have ever sailed in?

It is in the top three of all questions asked of seafaring captains on first meeting. My answer varies depending on the person asking the question, my mood, which story I wish to retell and how much energy I wish to invest in sharing it. One thing that affects all weather as a seafarer is the size and type of vessel, overlaid with the speed and the direction in which you seek to sail. What could feel abhorrent sailing west may be a pleasant downwind day heading east. The size of swells is often less important than the length between successive crests, and whether it is a clean single swell or multiple swells competing with each other. This diversity of situations only adds to the fascination. By answering the question, I also have the chance to in some way relive the day, the weather, the feeling. Some can evoke beautiful memories and others make me shudder.

Shuddering is a good point to start, as it was a shudder through the yacht that woke me from a faux sleep at 1am. Of course, the story had started much earlier, with our guests having a fantastic afternoon at the Soggy Dollar Bar on the island of Jost Van Dyke in the British Virgin Islands. It is a ramshackle place that draws in budget sailors and global icons. This time we delivered the latter: in our tender to the beach bar were a talk-show host, two multi-platinum-selling recording artists and several behind-the-scenes power brokers of the music industry. In the second tender were ten children belonging to the group, accompanied by their nannies and security staff.

We recovered our guests in various states of dishevelment just before sunset. The children returned first, the housekeeping team sending them to shower and remove the kilos of sand they had tracked into the yacht from the white beach on Jost Van Dyke. The adults returned in two groups: their identities had been uncovered by some of the other beach bar guests and the second group were delayed drinking the Dark & Stormies that had been bought for them by the delighted 'normal' patrons. The guests were having a blast, but I was watching the weather. The Caribbean is often windy and more than often rough, with 1- to 2-metre steep-sided waves. The passage we had to make that night was a full night underway across an exposed sea, and for weeks I'd been worrying about it.

All superyacht captains know the risk of open ocean night passages with their guests on board. The promise of the yachting adventure is that we will move daily to the next unique destination, but we will do so without anyone sensing the move. As simple as this goal seems, it discounts the folly of the ocean. Before leaving Jost Van Dyke in falling light, the wind and the seas were up and I knew it was less than ideal. We made ground to pass between Tortola and St John, and I slowed to savour the shelter of Tortola while the guests continued their party dinner. There was no rush and we 'idled' along in the lee of the island for three hours.

One of the smaller boats we carried was a 16-metre sports cruiser. It was complicated and time-consuming to lift so we often towed it as we relocated through the night. It had been modified for this and generally followed very well. I knew from the short passage across to Smuggler's Cove from Jost Van Dyke that tonight was not the night for towing, but the show goes on and I just hoped something might go in my favour. It was shortly before midnight when the guests went to their cabins. I waited a further 30 minutes before leaving the comfort of Tortola's barrier to the seas, hoping they would be asleep in this time. As soon as we cleared the island we were exposed to the west and started lifting with the seas – not dangerous, but certainly uncomfortable for the guests. We had a further line of islands that would give us some shelter before we were fully exposed for seven hours. We then had Anguilla and St Maarten to break the seas before our destination.

It wasn't great, but I needed to rest. I told the officer of the watch to use some discretion and adjust our heading and speed within a defined range to reduce movement. It seemed my head had just touched the pillow when the officer rang.

'You better come up. It's not good.'

That sort of call is why I sleep in trackpants and a T-shirt at sea. I was on the bridge 15 seconds later. The night camera was directed at the sports cruiser. It was a white spec among the many more 'white horses', the wind-driven breaking waves. I could see the waves crashing over the boat constantly, the tow line pulling the bow high into the air and then disappearing behind the next trough. The screen was riveting, I could not stop watching; any moment I expected the boat (worth US$1.5 million) to be swamped and just sink. I had the officer station a deckhand near the tow line on the yacht, with an axe to cut the 36mm tow line if sinking was the outcome.

An hour passed and the weather continued to deteriorate. We adjusted our heading and speed, but nothing changed our movement. The primary guest within the group was a true delight and so respectful to the crew, but a darker form came to the bridge to ask very pointedly if his family and friends were safe: I was able to reassure him that they were. I repeated my own thoughts to him – it was uncomfortable but not dangerous. He was not well from the movement, and I accept that feeling this way will test anyone's good nature. Sensing illness approaching, he departed quickly, retreating to the lower deck and his cabin.

All yachts and ships have support companies ashore and I rang ours. They were in Europe and the time zone meant it was a reasonable time for my call. I opened with the situation, stated my fatigue and that I knew I might not be seeing everything clearly. My main concern was pollution: if the sports cruiser sank, or the tow parted and drifted, it would release some of its 3,000 litres of petrol somewhere in the Caribbean. I asked the office to research and prepare all that was needed in case of this eventuality. My shore-based colleague sounded puzzled: 'Why do you want to sink the tender?' Keeping as close to calm as I could, I responded that whether the tender sank or not was largely out of my control now. We were in the middle of a night passage and needed to keep going. He still did not seem to fully understand but assured me the paperwork would be ready if needed.

The paperwork wasn't needed. We made it and once in the shelter of St Maarten and in daylight, we again slowed and brought the tow in close. One of the crew jumped in and, crazily, the engines started, and the boat was no worse for the journey. This is not even an especially dramatic bad weather story, just a glimpse of what a bit of complacency can bring. For 'real weather', it is necessary to go back a few years and down to the south.

We were in the Southern Ocean and pounding into a head sea on the Elliott-designed racing yacht *Mad Max*. It was the annual Sydney Hobart Yacht Race and as predictable as the rum at the finish were the brutal southerly conditions we were encountering. When racing in a storm there is no sense of hygiene, no sense of wet and dry, and no sense of sleep and waking. We were in survival mode on a small yacht in a big, angry ocean.

The media and sponsors gravitate to the majesty of the large yachts racing for line honours, and the sailing community acknowledges these machines for their greatness, but it is the smaller yachts that evoke the passion. At 12 metres, *Mad Max* was in the latter group and better suited for a day sail on Sydney Harbour than the Southern Ocean. It was a wide, flat and fast boat made for flying downwind. We were not downwind now, and as the seas built in two or three directions it was hard to determine the dominant swell. The wind moved around south and increased to 45 knots with only more threatening clouds on the horizon and the barometer falling rapidly.

We were a crew of eight and we knew each other well. We had raced together as a team for some time and knew our strengths and our limitations. We were not professional racers, but we were good amateurs and normally we maintained our swagger in the face of any conditions. The yacht's owner put his head above the cabin companionway and in a very calm voice said, 'Come off the wind boys, let's get downwind.' It seemed counter-intuitive as we were still racing, but such was the respect for the yacht's owner and our knowledge of each other that we moved as one to bear away from the wind. Within two minutes the world had changed: we were now running with the wind, reversing our previous heading, and it was eerily peaceful.

I had gone to the foredeck during the yacht's change of direction and was just moving back towards the cabin when the owner came fully into the cockpit to explain. The bolts holding the keel to the yacht were bouncing up and down and he did not know how long the keel would stay attached to the yacht. He did not say this before, as he needed us to execute the change of course as calmly as possible.

A collective fear gripped our small race crew. If the keel separated from the hull, the yacht would capsize and our chances of survival 60 miles from the coast in these conditions would be marginal. Conversation was sparse and to the point, movement around the yacht was cautious, and any adjustments to course or sails were heavily scrutinised by all on board. This continued for several hours, until the darkened line of the coast became more defined and by nightfall we arrived in Twofold Bay, Eden, on the New South Wales border with Victoria. There was a survivors' energy that night as we all realised we had lived to sail another day. I reflect on the calm the owner showed in the face of an imminent and life-threatening situation. Later, I will review fast and slow emergencies; the ability to stay calm in a rapidly evolving situation is the equivalent of slowing time, and equally as difficult. The yacht owner was not a professional mariner, he was a businessman who owned a sailboat, but he showed his poise at a time of great tension and I glimpsed who he was at his core and likely what had underwritten his business success.

Superyachts do not race, so there is no need to place the asset and its people at risk in the face of poor or deteriorating weather. This does not account for the situation where the yacht is somewhere less than ideal and cannot be somewhere else. Modern forecasting is exceptional and professional weather routers are my constant companions at sea by phone and email, but even with this support there remain variables and the ultimate responsibility for decisions relating to weather sits with the captain.

Crossing the Atlantic is a significant undertaking and doing so with multiple active hurricanes adds another layer of complexity. Without stepping into the troubled waters of global climate change, the spacing and intensity of Atlantic hurricanes has increased during my seafaring career to the point where they now seem to link hands across the ocean. On this occasion I was crossing in command of a very capable and seaworthy superyacht as the Category 5 Hurricane Dorian, one week ahead of our track, swept through the Bahamas, causing devastation and tragedy wherever it met human activity. Tropical Storm Gabrielle was also ahead of us, to the east and north of Dorian. A third system was further south and closer to our intended passage.

I looked at all the options and none were good. The third system was intensifying, and one prediction had it moving in the traditional path, in an arc to the north-west. The yacht was beginning to approach the dangerous northern quadrant and if the system sped up or bent to the north-east, we would not be able to outrun it. The yacht had recently suffered an engineering failure that had temporarily invoked a speed limitation. The fault was not truly rectified and if it repeated, we would be reduced to 5 knots, with no opportunity to move out of the way of the weather system.

I wrote lengthy briefings to my shoreside managers but there was no response of significance. As is always the case, I, as the captain, was on my own with only meteorologists as company. Two months prior to this Atlantic crossing I had read Rachel Slade's incredible book, *Into the Raging Sea: Thirty-three mariners, one megastorm, and the sinking of* El Faro. The failings of the captain, the crew and their shore team that sunk the *El Faro* raced through my mind, along with the lessons learned: check and cross-reference every weather source, stand strong in the face of timeline pressure and, most importantly, remember that hurricanes do not follow models. All 81 findings made in the official investigation and detailed in the book were rolling through my troubled mind as the barometer fell and the seas built. I did not sleep that night, preferring to constantly monitor all weather sources and manually plot the passage of the centre of the weather system. Sharing my thoughts with the officer on watch and the chief officer was valuable, though I knew that all their commentary could only support, not make, the decision for me. I had two levers to pull, neither very long when viewed against the size and capacity for a hurricane to change against its predicted path. I could alter course, I could alter speed, or I could and likely would engage a combination of both.

By morning, with the weather now at Beaufort Force 7 and increasing, all models and observed weather confirmed the hurricane remained to the south and would not intersect the yacht's path. I increased our speed and adjusted the yacht's heading 30 degrees to the north to place as much distance between the system and the yacht as possible. Over the next 12 hours, as the wind, seas and risk abated, I reflected on how close we had come to disaster without anyone ever knowing. I reduced speed to economical, returned the heading to the direct course, and the yacht continued the ocean crossing to Miami with fair weather. The morning after arrival, I was scrolling through the routine maritime alerts that are sent automatically to all ships. Even in port the Global Maritime Distress Signal System remains active, and I slumped back against the radio room bench as I read of the sinking of the ocean-going tug *Bourbon Rhode*, which was not as lucky as we were and had intersected with the same system, now named Hurricane Lorenzo. I followed the story over subsequent days to discover only three of the eleven crew had survived. There is a reason I obsess over weather.

There are many more times spanning the Pacific, Indian and Southern oceans where my humility has been reinforced in the face of the overwhelming force of nature. The many times that required me to grapple with contradictory information and make timely decisions sent me on a journey towards understanding how to make better decisions.

Weather and seafaring as a metaphor

The hurricane represents life: it cannot be controlled, and it is unlikely to follow the path you thought it would.

As a leader, as a citizen just seeking to cross your own ocean, you must gain information from as many sources as possible and challenge each one.

Learn what levers you have to embrace or avoid an event and seek counsel from diverse sources when you can.

Making better decisions

B roader than just dealing with weather, I knew that captaincy would require me to make decisions more frequently, and that those decisions would be more complex. It intrigued and then annoyed me that while decisions were being demanded of me all day, every day, I had not received any instruction in how to improve my decision-making. I began to try and close this gap by researching and trying to understand how and why I made decisions. In my everyday work this would improve my performance, but in extreme situations my making better decisions would potentially save lives at sea.

A doctor of medicine is required to make decisions and execute a strategy when a patient presents with a challenging case. They will look to a manual of reference where similar cases are recorded and review successful strategies to resolve the situation. The doctor can also study peer-reviewed papers for even more ideas and refer the patient to a specialist in exactly that area to truly round out their strategy for the patient's treatment. If the case challenges ethics as well, there will be a board of colleagues to further ensure the path chosen is correct. None of these steps are random: they will follow a decision pathway documented by the hospital, agreed by the state and made clear to the patient and their family. A decision is reached by design, not by errant judgement.

This clear path was not available when I began as a superyacht captain, but I did need some sort of basis for my decision-making, so in the absence of anything else I built it myself. It began as a collection of notes in a folder, progressed to an iPad, and then returned to a nicer leather-bound, plastic-sleeved notebook after the time the iPad battery was depleted and I needed information to correctly react to a fire. Core components included many technical details of the yacht, which I could look at during an emergency, and scripts for me to use when providing updates on the public address system. I was never confident making announcements, so this helped immensely, and I also built a series of flow charts that followed the simple path of 'If this happens, then what?' It was a decision support system to allow my relaxed rational self to lead in a crisis. It was universally recognised by the deck officers and referred to as Brendan's Magic Folder.

It reflected by omission the knowledge I held and, more importantly, covered what I was lacking. I had been doing this for some time and had used all the information in real situations: the effort in curating the magic folder was validated in my reality and then further when I saw a quote from the great Charlie Munger:

'Well, the first rule is that you can't really know anything if you just remember isolated facts and try and bang 'em back. If the facts don't hang together on a latticework of theory, you don't

have them in a usable form. You've got to have models in your head. And you've got to array your experience both vicarious and direct on this latticework of models. You may have noticed students who just try to remember and pound back what is remembered. Well, they fail in school and in life. You've got to hang experience on a latticework of models in your head.'

This quote was never written for captaincy, it was Munger reflecting on his own experiences, but it just rang so true for me. I have heard myself and my peers say, 'after 30 years at sea I have seen most things and through this I have an arsenal of solutions.' But time in itself is not enough. Yes, many events do have the same beat and past experience helps. But what if my actions in the past were flawed and my success was *in spite of* my actions? Will I just repeat the same errors? Will I reinforce poor decisions over and over until I am so enamoured with my choices that I am closed to alternative solutions? Like Munger points out, we need models to work with to hang our problems on and see them flow through to resolution and be prepared to do that again and again.

Models are not complex; they are frames to view challenges and speed up the process of getting to solutions. This is a prompt to do some further reading – it is worthwhile. I took this path, and along the way I learned the language and reference points. I learned to recognise my own confirmation bias, and it is significant. I seek information that will support my existing assumptions. I realised there was a term for circle of competence, and I would be well served to stay within it. Another favourite, which I found so valid for superyacht captaincy, was the inversion model. Instead of seeking brilliance, I tried to avoid catastrophe. This sounds so obvious, but until I read it I did not see the frame that helped me to protect 'the downside'. In finance this is well known, but I was responsible for lives, often in the middle of large oceans, and it had never been taught to me.

This is not my journey into business doublespeak, but a nod to the benefit I gained from learning the terms for events that were happening around me. Words and language matter. Without the language and awareness of mental models, I would not have identified when I grew through my imposter complex and enjoyed a brief moment of calm before realising I was now exposed to the 'competency trap'. A trap that held firm the belief that my experience and past success remained valid and would ensure success into the future: just play the same tune and the crowd will keep dancing. This doesn't work and I was lucky to see it in others as I may not have seen it in myself. Just as my workplace evolved from sextants to satellites, I had to also make sure that my decision-making was not static. I think my resting place has become: Read, Learn, Practise, Grow, Repeat. Following this cycle, I realised that even information I thought would be static, such as my core values, has evolved with time, experience and knowledge. My leadership style has changed immensely,

I hope for the better and am aided by maturity. Even with an avid interest in listening and reading on business and maritime in general, I was acutely aware that all knowledge has a use-by date and my learning wheel must keep rolling.

Making decisions

Decision-making will define your leadership, yet it is mostly ignored in education.

Learning the language for your decisions is essential.

There is no finish line: deeply held learning needs to be challenged, renewed and, if appropriate, discarded.

A defining moment

I do know that my experiences represent growth points and, like any weightlifter will share, to grow muscles you must tear, rebuild and tear again. Along this path there will be some moments of pain. My leadership growth involved many tears and repairs, and it has shaped who I have become along the way. As painful as many of these points have been, I would not have been able to move forwards without them. If I was to find a ground zero, I would have to go way back to my earliest times after qualifying from the navy. I lived through a great example of successful leadership, possibly the greatest 'tear and repair' moment of my personal growth. It charts a strategy by a very successful naval captain that became a defining moment in my career – one I would draw upon throughout my professional life.

It was 1994 and I was the senior officer of the watch (OOW) in a Royal Australian Navy frigate. The ship was 136 metres long, a terrifyingly narrow 14 metres wide and with a dead weight of 4,200 tonnes. The crew operating this ship varied between 210 and 220 officers and sailors, a high number for the size of ship, but this acknowledges the many specialists in a military operation. This frigate was enormous to me at the time, important to Australia's defence, and was referred to as a 'tier 1 warship' (not that I could ever have imagined it back then, but it was smaller than several of the yachts I would later command). Our ship was not the best performer, and we were aware of it, but at my level there was little to be done. In any case, I was having too much fun with life beyond the ship to care.

There was a change of captain and the ship went to sea for two weeks of assessment by the navy's training team, led by the Sea Training commander. This team was often referred to as 'the wreckers' or 'green team' in acknowledgement of their green jumpsuits; the crew wore grey. The green team tested the frigate to its limits in all aspects of its performance; their assessment was professional, ahead of its time and brutal. There were simulated attacks, fires and floods and then it would all start again. It was relentless. The Sea Training commander was one of those barrel-chested shorter men who seemed to move with purpose, even when the purpose was hard to discern.

This 'chief wrecker' was known to me – he had delivered a soaring lecture on the importance of 'Rules of Engagement' in my final year at the Defence Academy, pacing the dais of the lecture hall where 150 cadets sat riveted to his every word. He had no microphone, and none was needed as he retold the story of boarding a suspected illegal immigrant vessel in the waters between Indonesia and Australia. When he spoke of stepping across onto the boat, he stomped on the stage; when he retold his commands to the crew on the boarded vessel, he barked them to the lecture hall, in English and Bahasa Indonesian no less. There was a crescendo building in his tale, and it came with him yelling to nobody in particular in the lecture hall, 'Stop or I will shoot!' and again, still louder, 'Berhenti atau aku akan Menembak!'

Then came silence from the stage as he stood square to the audience, arms raised in a shooter's stance, a gruelling 20 seconds: he was a polished performer. We needed to know, what happened? The proverbial pin would have been deafening. And then, with one arm now outstretched, he said quietly, 'and he just ran in the other direction'. He screamed the order again and still he ran, so he did what he had to do – he shot, and accidentally took off half of one of the skipper's ears with a bullet meant to go metres above. Since this lecture, I have never forgotten the importance of rules of engagement in any setting. When you call 'Stop or I will shoot!', regardless of what the shooting represents metaphorically, there is no way back: you must pull the trigger when they do not stop.

As this ear-shooting senior officer careered around the ship, I did my best to keep out of his arc of destruction. In contrast to the bustle of the Sea Training commander, our new captain seemed to move at a slower pace. His middle name was known, used and was important. It was as though he slowed time to allow passers-by to be able to think through all his names. He was tall and rangy, with hair that was militarily correct, but not so much that it denied his personality the chance to shine. He was possibly the first person I had met with real presence. In a military that was all about uniformity, he stood out: whether it was his speech or his precise manner of walking, there was no way of mistaking that he was the leader. As junior officers, we paid homage to his speech by trying to recreate his tonal mannerisms. If we had been overheard it may have seemed that we were mocking, but we weren't: we were mimicking out of respect, trying to learn our own styles. His charisma had us all enthralled. The captain brought some trusted senior members with him and with their influence he turned the ship's performance around. The ship came through the assessment strongly, better than ever before, with some real compliments from the normally dour trainers. There was an upbeat feel to the ship's crew when we returned to port.

The captain debriefed his teams in small groups in his cabin. This was the Royal Australian Navy in 1994: group debriefs in the personal space of the captain's cabin were an exception to the point of being unheard of. This captain was shaking things up. He was bringing the navy forward and would place his own stamp on naval captaincy. The charismatic captain had moved through the departments providing his frank assessments of their performance. I had seen the engineers, the weapons officers and the communications officers all return to the wardroom. They huddled and spoke in hushed tones to absorb what had been shared. It was clear this new captain was telling some home truths. The phone rang in the wardroom and the steward advised the navigator that his team was requested.

The navigation team consisted of three officers of the watch, four assistant OOW and a navigating officer. Within this group, I was the senior of the OOW by experience and longevity on board.

Growing up in and around boats and racing sailing dinghies gave me an advantage: the bridge environment was more natural to me. My peers were under great strain and some were buckling under a combination of fatigue, brutal admonishment for small errors and performance pressure to manoeuvre the ship in accordance with instructions. A daily event was officer of the watch manoeuvres, where the ships would gather in a group and move around each other under the direction of the senior ship – synchronised swimming with ships is the best way I can describe this. It taught young officers how to take bold action to swiftly relocate to another position relative to one of the other ships. It was not uncommon for the juniors to find themselves physically ill prior to these manoeuvres, due to the intense pressure placed upon them by the navigators and the captains. The navy has come a long way since this time and are leading educators today, but back then it was more about survival. I shared the fatigue, but I looked forward to the manoeuvres – they were fun, and I treated them like a start sequence in a sailing race. I was 23 years old and employed to play with these racehorses of the sea for up to three hours a day. It was clear I was confident in this environment and my competence was recognised by my peers, who would shuffle to stand behind me when a tricky manoeuvre was on offer, whereas I would step forward and engage. Or so I thought.

The navigator led the small team into the captain's cabin. There was the due formality of greeting the senior officer, but the assessment had been completed and with it the pressure of the past weeks had eased. The navigator had an infectious, cheeky grin and he greeted the captain buoyantly, and this was returned with the captain sharing a warm and conspiratorial moment with the navigator. They knew they had turned the performance of the ship around and sent the Sea Training group back to Maritime Headquarters in Sydney singing the praises of our performance. The captain ceded the gathering to the navigator, who began mechanically with a list of the events that had been completed successfully during the past weeks. He included supportive comments from the fleet navigating officer, who had asked for his compliments to be passed on. As a navigation team we had been assessed on our ability to overcome breakdowns, respond to simulated man overboard drills, communicate for the ship during major fire or flooding exercises and of course handle the ship during the officer of the watch manoeuvres and combined anti-submarine exercises.

After this, the captain thanked the navigator and praised him in front of the team for his bridge leadership: this was well deserved and acknowledged by all. He then further noted the improved performance he had observed in the weeks since joining, and restated the expectation he had voiced on his first day when he held a full ship's company meeting, this being that we were to be the best ship in the navy. There were no other expectations. His brief was as clear as it was succinct. He then drew attention to the lack of experience and poor ship familiarity of some of the junior members of the bridge and said that they must work harder. I was just out of the captain's direct eyeline and was nodding knowledgeably to the points he was making: these junior OOW needed to work harder. I could see this and only just stopped short of speaking up in agreement.

As we were in his cabin and seating was limited, I had straddled the arm of a sofa, respectfully so, but I was definitely showing my ease in this ship. My view of self was nicely defined, I was well liked, blessed with a (little) natural ability on the bridge and was ready to step off that evening to pick up my social life ashore with the rugby club, a life that I held more important than any workplace responsibilities. The captain moved quickly in tone as he said the shortcomings of the junior team were not a concern to him: the ship was about to conduct an extended tour to the Indian and Pacific oceans and end with a circumnavigation of Australia. There would be more than enough time to learn. What did concern him was attitude. A poor attitude was poisonous, and negativity would not be tolerated. OK, fair point I thought, but what's the relevance? The next ten minutes remain somewhat of a blind spot in my memory as the captain turned towards me with a withering review and dismantling of my performance, so that my errors seemed to magnify to a point where I shared his view that I was not worthy of setting foot on his bridge, or any bridge. He built his monologue into a guided and managed fury that I had never experienced before and have not since.

It seems my practised ease was not compatible with the captain's goals and that of the navy he believed in. The message was: pick it up or pack it up, and as a first step I could take the weekend watch duties as time towards some first thoughts on how to improve. The navigation team was dismissed, and in a daze I followed (or was led by others) out of the cabin. I had just been struck down in front of my peers and I could see by my fellow junior officers' aversion to catching my eye that they too had been blindsided by my downfall. Only hours previously I had been their peer-mentor and had been helping them through the intricacies of their own bridge performance. I had thought this support had been sought and welcomed, but now I wasn't sure. Had they only been humouring me all along, also knowing that I was a somewhat 'lame duck' bridge performer?

In the weeks and months that followed, I worked harder than I ever had. I began seeking new knowledge and challenging any accepted practice that could be improved. I would never be the 'straight down the line' navy guy, I valued my personal freedoms a little too much, but I would be the best I could within these limitations. I enjoyed that others began to seek my input, as opposed to before my downfall, when I gave my opinion freely. I recovered my loss of face with my colleagues in the navigation team just by the sheer weight of work I took on. All the while, the captain barely acknowledged my existence. I began to realise this was just how it would be. I would be on the bridge and the captain, in a jovial voice, would greet the junior signals sailor by his first name and make a joke on some topic of the day. He and the navigating officer were very tight and there was always laughter in their conversation. In contrast, the limited conversations with me were questioning and factual in nature: what is the speed, course of another ship, anticipated weather? My first name was never used and nothing more than a perfunctory 'thank you' was received.

Many months later, somewhere between Singapore and Hong Kong, there had been a need to dive on the hull. As the ship's diving officer, I led the team and was required to brief the captain and gain his approval before we entered the water. Time was short and after deliberation I thought I would save time if I conducted the brief in a wetsuit, dry, but not the uniform an officer should be wearing on the bridge to brief the captain. I was nervous approaching the bridge, I was hot in the wetsuit and feeling immense pressure due to the limited time in restricted navigation available for the dive on the hull. The captain looked me up and down in the wetsuit and with a huge smile said, 'Would you look at that, the diver does seal impersonations.' He laughed and signed the dive sheet without a second glance. 'Have a good dive, Brendan, and keep your team safe.' I had not heard him say my name in nearly a year, and it took a moment to realise he was speaking to me and handing the dive checklist back with a broad grin.

From this point, my time on the outside was over: the captain sought my input, allowed my humour (at times) and referred others to seek my counsel to find solutions on challenging problems. I never slackened back to my former self – I knew the gift he had given could just as quickly be taken away. He had lifted me from a lackadaisical young officer to one that was hard-working and professional. I may never have made the 'best OOW the navy had seen' but after those years I was truly 'the best OOW I could have been'. That horrible day in 1994 stays with me and I have drawn upon it many times to focus my efforts into my own captaincy. I take nothing for granted and realise that my own success pivots entirely on my application and not through a divine aptitude for seafaring.

Through my personal fascination with studying leadership, I observed that this captain was clearly the archetypal 'charismatic leader'. By sheer force of personality, he drew the most from all those around him, me very much included. Through my years of always hoping to become a successful captain, I often thought of his approach. It was not an approach available to me as it wasn't suited to my personality and would have been a poor imitation. I would have to find my own journey and suffer the errors along the way. For my captain, it was truly his authentic self and it worked at all levels. I cannot say that I would have sought his company for friendship, even if we were peers, though I worked harder under his leadership than I ever knew I could. He taught me a great lesson, and

I can only be thankful that I learned it early enough in my career to benefit from it.

I am not brushing over the feelings I had in the time immediately after the meeting in the captain's cabin. I mourned the loss of my own self-assessed competence; I lost my confidence, and it took time to move across this dip. In a more aware time, I would have sought support from peers or professionals. I was very weak for some time.

Feedback

Feedback can be painful, poorly delivered and is always subject to another's perception of you. Nevertheless, it is the most valuable information you have access to. Treasure it, challenge it, grow with it.

Ahead of starting in any workplace, we all have visions of how we will perform, who we will be and what our expectations are of our employer. Consider noting these and referring to them at intervals during your employment.

Check in with what you are feeling now in the job: how does this compare to what you thought you would feel? How and what can you do to return to that pre-commencement vision? This is your feed-forward to reach the heights you hoped to before the daily noise of the workplace drowned this signal out.

A personal board of directors

The three years at the Australian Defence Force Academy and then the additional year at the naval college were arduous. It was a time where physical and mental harassment were seen as a rite of passage, and those of us who finished the training – fewer than 50 per cent – had developed a resilience. There was no choice, as during this time we had been screamed at, drained by fatigue, ridiculed in front of our peers and made to feel inferior. Those doing this were not manifestations of any wickedness, just reflecting the doctrine of the time.

I survived well as a first-year cadet, largely because I kept my mouth shut in front of my seniors and played Australian Rules Football: the two combined were enough to give me easier passage than many of my peers. I was proud when I and a classmate were singled out for a resilience competition. For my challenge I was held down, a wet cloth over my face, water poured on until I gagged. This technique would later be made famous by the US military in post-9/11 years and we would all learn the term 'waterboarding'. I remember seeing the headlines and being taken back to my first year and I felt great sympathy for those being interrogated; it really is awful.

Concurrently, to test who could withstand which challenge the longest, my year mate was locked in a cupboard with a toaster, the burning bread removing the oxygen until he passed out. When released, and after we both recovered, we laughed it off – it was something we went through together; we couldn't be broken. I am going to say for historical record that I lasted longer with the water than Junior with the toaster, but I am always going to say this; I cannot recall.

Learning this power of camaraderie early on led to my always seeking a trusted group. I may no longer have access to the group of mischievous cadets that I once roamed with, though I have recreated the support over time and with a conscious focus on quality over quantity.

Developing a layered circle to support me has been crucial. I have long since let go of the idea that I have a sixth sense for weather, an innate aptitude for navigation, or that the award of a captain's licence somehow made me infallible. As captain I am required to show a consistently strong countenance, but I am under no illusion that I can go it alone. Luckily, I never have been alone in my captaincy: my personal board of advisors are with me always. Even when we are out of direct contact, I can channel their perspective.

Yvonne has at all times been there to answer the phone and just listen when I have been away at sea. Even when she was raising our two daughters, Fabienne and Scarlett, as infants, her sleep broken and her days completely taken over by child-rearing, Yvonne was always there to affirm that I was better than I thought I was, and that I would make the correct choices. I knew many times that she would be saying this without listening to the situation I was trying to retell. It didn't really matter: she was there unconditionally.

Not equal to Yvonne but just as present in my career has been my best mate, Wes. Everyone I have sailed with knows of Wes through my random stories that involve him. Through these anecdotes, I introduce him as the most famous person in yachting never to have been in yachting. Whereas Yvonne is unconditionally supportive, Wes is unconditionally challenging. One of the two of us will often start with: 'I need my unreasonable friend.' What follows will be a brutally critical assessment of the situation and our performance, with the insight only lifelong friendship can deliver. We assess situations without glossing over the ugly parts of our actions. I have left calls with Wes shaken as he intelligently and knowingly squeezes lemon into the self-supporting assumptions I had built for my own comfort. His rationality is precise as he dismantles the emotional filter I develop through my association with the yacht, its owner and the crew, to return the facts boxed in the same headers we always use: 'The Good, The Bad, The Ugly.' These headers allow uncomfortable information to be shared with no recourse. We can praise unconditionally or punch hard with uncomfortable assessments of each other's actions, all within a pre-agreed frame. It protects the friendship as we never take offence, it is what these calls are for, and we tackle our personal and professional challenges with the benefit only informed candour can provide.

The third member of my troika is Malcolm. My former captain when I was learning my way through yachting, Malcolm now provides me with technical guidance. In my early years, if André taught me the 'why' of yachting, Malcolm taught me the 'how'. Malcolm's technical proficiency, insatiable thirst for new knowledge, awareness of his professional obligations and willingness to learn and adapt new technologies remain an inspiration and an aspiration. That he was a patient educator when we sailed together, providing an accelerated learning environment, is just icing on a large cake.

Malcolm moved effortlessly between the courteous well-spoken host for guests and the quick-witted crew member enjoying banter. It was his natural manner, and with his unrivalled technical competence the yacht owner and the crew relaxed with his command. Malcolm would not be found in the bars holding court with his or other crew – while this is a well-trodden path for many captains seeking to bolster their social currency, it was not for Malcolm. Malcolm's example set a high bar as I began to shape and define my own approach.

It was Malcolm's example during my period sailing as first officer that gave me an understanding of how the Mediterranean 'fitted together'. Malcolm showed me how best to set an anchor on the approach to Pampelonne Beach, adjacent to Saint-Tropez, so the yacht would not be compromised when the weather changed. He would point out the other yachts that had not taken such precautions and would be in trouble later in the afternoon. There was humble satisfaction when his guests continued to enjoy their day as other yachts scrambled to relocate. He shared relationships with port officials in Italy whose blessing was needed to secure the best docks, and when in Spain he stepped through the complex permit obligations with ease, making sure I understood each action.

Ship handling to Malcolm was a passion that he wished to share. It began by anchoring with precision and progressed to port departures, and eventually the holy grail: port arrivals. In my future, I would adopt this layered approach many times when mentoring deck officers and chief officers. I would introduce the ship-handling journey they were about to embark on by speaking of a captain I sailed with who would expect me to anchor with the precision of docking and dock with pre-defined metrics to guide me; I can only hope I have carried the legacy satisfactorily. Above all, what I gained from my observations of Malcolm was that there is just no shortcut for research and learning. You cannot experience all weathers in all locations, but you can research more to cover your gaps. Sailing the world, I would apply Malcolm's principles and heighten my already inquisitive nature to seek knowledge from anyone and at any time.

Even with this emotional and professional support gained from Yvonne, Wes and Malcolm, I still never felt fully informed about the day-to-day demands of captaincy around the globe. I augmented my knowledge with a select group of crew, the core based not on rank but those with whom I could form a bond. They formed my counsel and filled my blind spots.

In my first captaincies, one of my blind spots was around my manner: I felt I had an easy leadership style that welcomed communication and, luckily, I never heard criticism or concerns. What a lovely bubble I lived in. It was to burst when I employed a frank Cornish farmer's daughter, who told it to me straight: I was aloof, fickle in mood and it was very clear, within a crew of 40, that I had favourites. Apparently, I cast a long shadow and crew realised the easiest path was to go along with any suggestion I made. This might read as very familiar in a traditional top-down leadership situation, but aside from being poor leadership, it is downright dangerous in an operational environment. There is no way to promote and embrace open communications if it doesn't start with the captain. I espoused all virtues of open communications but risked being an empty vessel by not living it through my actions.

None of this I was aware of or felt in any way represented my lived experience to that point. But this 'inside truth' from a trusted colleague made me rethink my behaviour and strategies. I could not just believe in my own assumptions. I improved, I spoke strongly in support of the challenge culture on the bridge and throughout the yacht and many times provided a living example. As with any leader, I continued to have blind spots and needed emotional and professional support, and I would continue to rely on my counsel to help address them.

Sage counsel

Great leaders are often a representation of great support.

Whether it was my captain in 1994, my best friend or a trusted colleague, I learned, sometimes painfully, never to be too confident that my view of self was what was shared by the wider world.

Build your own advisory board and take from and give to in equal measure.

Is that the Prince?

After extolling the virtues of soliciting honest and challenging feedback, I confess I still had lapses. 'Lapses' is me being kind to myself; there were times in my need to please when I barrelled on regardless of the wisdom provided by the truth-tellers I had surrounded myself with.

We were back in the South of France after passage from the Indian Ocean via the Suez Canal, and anchoring off Saint-Jean-Cap-Ferrat I felt we had returned. I know the area intimately, having anchored here hundreds of times, and when Yvonne and I lived in Nice we often took walks around the point, stopping for a swim in one of the secluded bays. It felt great as I looked to the view to the west, across villas I knew well on the headland, from the bridge of a wonderful superyacht. It was a 100-metre-plus yacht with over 40 crew and licensed to carry 36 guests in open seas. Its delivery marked a shift in the yachting industry, shaking some perceptions with its more rugged approach, and I was proud of this captaincy.

This yacht-owning couple referred to me as the senior captain, a term that does not specifically mean anything – it alluded to my now decades' experience with complex captaincies. Regardless of its lack of definition, I was conscious of their expectation and tried to set a sound example and freely share the benefit of my experience with more junior crew. On this evening, experience was not really needed: there was a visibly solid ground swell running offshore and a strong south-westerly wind, creating a confused sea. The anchorage at Saint-Jean-Cap-Ferrat was an obvious choice as being the most sheltered. The yacht owners were on board and, more importantly, some of their most favoured guests had made a point of arranging a dinner booking in Monaco to provide a special evening in gratitude for the kindness of the owners in sharing the yacht with them.

We made preparations to depart Saint-Jean-Cap-Ferrat to move towards Monaco and my nervous anxiety was building. It wasn't helped when the ever friendly and professional French port pilot boarded and said, 'But Captain, why would you go to Monaco now? It is terrible and getting worse.' I rolled my eyes: 'Thanks, Pilot, I know.' I had told the guests that Monaco might be uncomfortable but, in a good mood, they wanted to try anyway. They did not wish to drive along the winding, single-lane Basse Corniche from Saint-Jean port all the way to Monaco during peak hour. I agreed the drive would be slow and, against my better judgement, I said that we would work something out for them: after all, I wanted them to see me as the successful superyacht captain.

It is worth departing from the events that are soon to unfold to expand on the guests that evening. 'Perfect' may be too great for any one group to live up to, but from a captain's and crew's point of view they certainly came close. It included an icon of the music industry who had, over four decades, released as many hits as any, and played with everyone worthy of sharing a stage with. There was also the enigmatic CEO and his wife, who gushed over every crew member's efforts on their behalf, their children having won the yacht over with their playful mischievousness. Sometimes guests at this level place unreasonable pressure on those around them through the force of their will. In this case, it was quite the opposite. These guests were adaptable, and they would have accepted the weather for what it was. I was the one who created the pressure by not wanting to let them down: I sought to please and deliver on the dream that yachting can be.

Many superyacht captains define themselves by their ability to deliver the seemingly impossible, and in doing so spin a web of pressure around themselves and the teams they lead. This pressure stems from the often unspoken tension in the relationship between captain and yacht owner: the captain is legally responsible, yet everyone knows the yacht owner is in charge – at least, until he is not. It is a confronting moment when the yacht owner, who on a normal day is the true Master of their Universe and not used to following anyone's direction, least of all an employee, is given a firm 'No' by the captain. No due to safety, no due to limitations of yacht or crew or no due to a breach of the captain's ethical code. I have had many 'no' conversations and each is preceded with a sense of dread, executed with apprehension and followed up with cautious reflection. On this night I did not say no and, as the evening unfolded, the pressure of not doing this became evident first to me and then, as the pace and complexity of events evolved, it radiated outwards to the team.

The move from the Saint-John-Cap-Ferrat anchorage to Monaco is not long, though through a combination of geography and meteorology within this busy stretch of the French coast the weather can be very different across 5 miles. On this night it certainly was, and the Monaco anchorage didn't look promising. There were seven yachts visible and a couple more that could be seen on the radar.

Instinctively, I sought my binoculars to look at the movement of the other yachts in the anchorage. Since the wind was out of the south-west and the yacht was heading north-east, there was an uneasy calm: we were 'running' with the sea and the wind and it made for a comfortable trip. I could imagine the guests, still at the lunch table, speaking to each other about their captain being overly concerned about the weather for no reason: 'It's lovely sailing along the coast.'

I often refer to sailing downwind as downhill and turning back to the wind as uphill. As a recreational cyclist, I am only too aware that for every kilometre freewheeling downhill there will be its equivalent grind in the return climb. As I scanned the horizon, it was clear the other yachts were pitching and rolling, and I wondered why they were staying there in such conditions. Even without guests, it would not have been comfortable. Among these yachts was a large cruise ship, which dominated the anchorage. Monaco and the French coast are heavily trafficked by cruise vessels and while the locals speak out against them, they cannot turn away the revenue from the thousands of day guests that flock ashore and spend heavily in the coastal towns. This ship was the *Celebrity Edge*; at 306 metres long, it dominated the area. I do not hold great knowledge of the cruise industry, but even without talking to the deck officer on the bridge it was clear that this ship was new; it had aggressive modern lines and was built to its extremities to optimise income-generating areas.

The *Celebrity Edge* had a daring plumb bow and carried her superstructure unnaturally forward. I commented on this and the officer of the watch confirmed that the ship was on its maiden voyage and 'represented a new generation of passenger comfort'. I may not have agreed with this sales pitch, read from the cruise company's website, but I ached to have the stability and size they were displaying. The ship was using its dynamic positioning system to thrust against the sea and provide a safe boarding area for its 3,000 guests, all seeking to return having spent the day browsing memorabilia stores in Monaco and trying to find links between Monaco today and the Monaco of Princess Grace.

I knew given the wind and the sea that the ship would be using significant thrust to hold position and that this thrust would flatten the water on their lee side. I felt a plan brewing and while I rarely call other vessels on the VHF radio, I did on this occasion so that our close approach would not cause alarm. I asked the ship if they were intending to move as I would like to pass their stern at around 100 metres and then take position 60 metres on their downwind side but at 90 degrees to their heading. In other words, what I wanted to do was point our yacht at their middle and 'hide' in their protection (think sheltering behind a wall on a windy day). The ship had no issue with my plan; they were dealing with their own concerns. There were 2- to 3-metre swells tossing their boats recklessly as they tried to unload their passengers. My assumption was reinforced when I could see the glass bridge wing. There stood the captain, staff captain and others, all staring down at their boarding area. There was some form of gaudily painted gantry that raised and lowered, and again my deck officer came forward with the ship's website marketing spiel, informing us that this gantry was advertised as 'the Magic Carpet' that provided safer guest boarding. Looking at the faces on the bridge wing, I am not convinced they were feeling the magic...

Celebrity Edge's dynamic positioning was working very hard in the conditions, and as the yacht passed I felt the push and our heading changed 20 degrees. At 6,000 tonnes the yacht was a significant vessel, but with 55 megawatts of power available this cruise ship was pushing a torrent of water out the stern and to the side. Nevertheless, we made our way to the area I thought would be suitable for our own guest transfer, sadly without a magic carpet. We took up position and I was mightily proud of my planning. The cruise ship was as good a mobile breakwater as had ever been designed and we had a chance for a bit of calm. The officer of the watch and the chief officer were on the bridge and as we settled into position, I asked the chief officer to go and have a look at the transom. Was it safe for our guests to board the tenders?

I trusted the chief officer's judgement and also knew he erred a little more on the side of caution than I did. In the current conditions, this would not be a bad thing. The yacht was settling into its new location as our tenders caught up with us after their bruising journey across the bay. My preference is always to allow the small boat coxswains to exercise their best judgement when moving ahead or behind the yacht. What I can see from the bridge is often not reflected in what they are experiencing in the tenders. In this case, I was pleased with their choice to follow astern of the yacht, using the larger vessel to smooth the way.

There was a wide-angle camera installed to observe the boarding area of the yacht: we relied on it heavily and were aware that it distorted the image a little. Generally, it made things look better than they were, with the tenders not moving as much on camera as they did in reality. It gave me some concern as ahead of the chief officer's radio call I saw our 14-metre tender moving across the full arc of the camera's field of view. It would crest a swell and be in full view of the camera and then disappear from sight as it sank into the next trough. Even with *Celebrity Edge* helping, the ground swell remained. It was not an option to move our guests from here and I spoke on the radio ahead of the tender's first docking attempt to ask the driver to hold off. It was rare for me to pre-empt the opinion of the person on the spot, especially as it was the trusted chief officer, but since we all knew how much pressure there was on making the boarding a success, the abort needed to come from me.

It was 5pm and the guests were scheduled to be ashore by 6.15pm. I slumped back to my chair on the bridge in a funk; there was no time now to return to our previous anchorage where it was safe, and there was no chance of a transfer at sea here.

If I had managed expectations when talking hours ago with the guests and not sought to astonish them with my own performance, we would all be relaxed and enjoying the previous location and the evening ahead. I was increasingly aware that my seeking to please was risking the performance of my entire crew. The officer of the watch, more to make small talk than anything, pointed to a 50-metre motor yacht entering Monaco port and said, 'Shame we can't just do that.' I straightened in the chair as the lightbulb in my mind lit, and thanked him for the idea. He looked at me quizzically, and I quickly zoomed the electronic chart (ECDIS) to the port entry. There were many new restrictions in place due to the Larvotto extension building works over the sea adjacent to Monaco, but I wasn't too worried as I knew the port intimately. I was energised and excited, I had thought of a way to deliver my guest experience in the time frame available: I was going to be the Successful Superyacht Captain today. In this mood I am hard to sway and respond poorly to any negative energy. The chief officer returned to the bridge and in a defeated tone asked, what happens now?

I was excitedly on my feet and shared my plan. Indeed, the plan was being made up as I spoke it, so to call it a plan would do disservice to any plan ever made. We would nose into the shelter of the outer port, stop parallel to Quai Rainier III and discharge our guests. His body language and face did not reflect my excitement. I sensed this and to cover some ground I added, 'Of course it will be with the port's approval.' He asked, 'Will we take a pilot?' I said we would if the port requested one, but given it is just after five and our move was not scheduled, likely there will not be one available. If this is the case, we will go alone. To add motion and authenticity to my hastily assembled plan, I picked up the VHF radio handset and called the port. The voice answering was youthful, which pleased me. In my most polite and clear voice, I stated the yacht's name and call sign, and requested permission to enter the port. The youthful French port worker responded, 'Yes, hello, no problem.' I could see on the face of the chief officer he was not satisfied with this. In my reply, along with repeating the yacht's name and call sign, I added the size: 'Over 100 metres, beam 18 metres and could you please repeat confirmation.' His response showed some annoyance: 'Yes, I give you approval already.'

Now, I knew the radio operator speaking in his second language had missed the size of the yacht. The chief officer knew this also and I knew that he knew. Regardless, I was back on my plan and said, 'Send the tenders in ahead to get ready and let's line up for an entry.' The officer of the watch was nervous: he was sitting at the control station, and I knew this approach in these conditions was far beyond his skill and experience. I confirmed to him that I would take the controls, so there was no need to waste any more time. Normally an officer of the watch would be in a terrible mood with me if I took a port entry from them – in this instance, he was clear of the chair before I finished saying I would take control.

I am very diligent about an arrivals or departure brief. I value visualising the manoeuvre, identifying each officer's role and talking through emergency scenarios. It was clear from both the officer of the watch and the chief officer's manner that they were not comfortable with these normal practices being bypassed. There was pride in the way the bridge was managed, and I was the leading advocate for the approach we normally took, but on this day my zeal to meet client needs meant I sidestepped it all.

We made the approach, which over the years I had done many times before. Granted, it had been on smaller yachts, in better weather and with some planning, but it felt similar at least. We turned the familiar corner with the Fairmont Hotel on the headland to the north of the port; the northern outer breakwater, with the yacht designer Espen Øino's office on its end, was also to the north and now to the yacht's starboard side. To the east, our port side, was the Quai Rainier III. As we drew parallel with Quai Rainier III, the water calmed and the officer of the watch and the chief officer's demeanour visibly improved. The manoeuvre was executed without the normal planning and briefing but it had been safe, and we were now in a good position for our guests to disembark for their evening in Monaco.

What the others on the bridge did not realise is that while entering seemed difficult to them, it was the departure that was on my mind. Given the sea, it would not have been safe to depart astern into the swell, and I had assumed there would be room in the outer port to turn around. I had turned around in this area once before on a slightly smaller yacht, and this reference was all I had. With the haste of the entry, no plan and no pilot, I was not aware that the outer port was quite full of moored yachts also seeking shelter. The 100-metre yacht *Symphony* was docked facing us and had set their port anchor responsibly wide to provide security against the swell; this constrained the area to the south, our port side. The area in front of the Monaco Yacht Club was also heavily spoken for, with many yachts and an additional floating dock in place to cater for regatta yachts: this was our starboard side blocked.

At this point, nobody else was aware of this situation and there was a buoyant mood. The chief officer left the bridge to await the guests' departure. I asked him to speak with the yacht owner and pass on my apologies, but I would stay on the bridge: they would understand, as it was clear the yacht was very tight in the port. The guests were always a few minutes late, so I had the chance to run through the 'what happens next?' question that was in my thoughts and causing my foot to tap on the chair. Other crew had begun to realise where we were and the crew radio buzzed across the interior channel. 'Have a look outside, we're in Monaco' was the general flavour of the radio chatter. I used small adjustments of the engines to hold the yacht in a stationary position about 10 metres from the end of the Monaco Yacht Club welcome dock for about ten minutes and in this time our guests prepared to depart with their now very short and comfortable tender ride. During this pause I could see there was a black-tie event on the dock in front of the yacht club, with what looked like professional cameras flashing in front of a group of 20. It was the golden hour for lighting and I could see our guests on the aft deck cameras, phone cameras out, poses struck and their obvious pleasure at entering Monaco port in such style.

Moments after the guests had departed, the deck radio came to life with a report of an official-looking boat from the port approaching our transom telling us that we could not be here. I said to tell the boat to talk to the control tower, who had already authorised our manoeuvre. This was flimsy but seemed to work. The chief officer returned to the bridge and spoke of the guests being in good spirits. I thanked him and said it was time we left: we'd have to do the guest pick-up later in the night from the bay in Saint-Jean-Cap-Ferrat. It was very clear we had already outstayed our welcome. I took the chance to briefly apologise to both the chief officer and the officer of the watch for breaching our own protocols with the entry and reassured them that for the departure we would do much better. To their credit, they did not labour the ad hoc nature of the last manoeuvre and I think they appreciated the apology.

I continued my briefing on the departure by asking who had previously been inside Port Hercule, the inner old port of Monaco. Neither had. The chief officer asked why it mattered as we were just backing out the way we came, weren't we? I explained that we could not reverse out due to the sea, and we also could not turn around in the current position, so the only option was to continue through the old port walls and into Port Hercule proper. The officers' faces gave way from the gratitude of only moments before to an empty glazed expression as they looked ahead in a unison of disbelief into what seemed like a full port.

It is worth pointing out that in making my decision I drew upon my own experience of bringing similar-sized yachts into the inner harbour, and also that the 105-metre *Lady Moura* was once a firm feature docked in the middle of the T-jetty of the old port. The others did not know this and from the perspective of where we stood, it did not look promising to their eyes. To cover some of the concerns, I made clear that nothing would begin until all normal pre-departure checks were complete, and I also briefed on how I would manoeuvre within the port. With the guests off the yacht, I knew I needed to return some normalcy to operations to maintain the confidence of my deck officer colleagues.

I had now spent almost 15 minutes visualising the port and how the yacht would manoeuvre. It was easy to communicate this; we would enter at around 1½ knots, with a bias to the north. As soon as the stern reported they were clear to swing, I would drive the stern to the west, the yacht's port side, and pin the bow in place. I was not sure if the stern would have room to go all the way through the turn and I thought that at some point past 90 degrees I would be able to move the bow ahead or back towards the entry to give more room to turn if needed.

Monaco port has visiting yachts and those that are home-ported. It is common to refer to a location by the name of a home-ported yacht. In this case, it was the 70-metre yacht *Siran* that was important to the turn. *Siran* was docked on the northern edge of the inner quai and we would need to have the bow as close as possible to her to have a chance of making it through the turn. I identified *Siran* for the benefit of the others and explained it would represent our pivot point when we turned around the bow.

It was a perfunctory brief, and as I asked for any questions it was clear that nobody else had any idea how I was going to do this. In hindsight, while I may have briefed confidently, I too was not so sure the execution would be as smooth as the brief. No questions were forthcoming, so we began. I started moving ahead and the chief officer was professionally calling speeds and distances. Aside from the one unanswered question (will we fit?), everything was largely back into the rhythm that all were comfortable with. I glanced over my shoulder as I heard a whispered, 'This is really tight, isn't it?' and I noticed there were about 12 crew on the bridge to witness this port entry. It was not uncommon to have one or two crew on the bridge for port entry; it was encouraged as part of engendering a shared awareness of all that occurs on board, but 12 put a little performance anxiety into the mix if it did all go horribly wrong.

Just as we entered, the lack of planning caught up with us again. There was yet another additional floating dock to cater for the regatta yachts extending to precisely where only a couple of minutes earlier I had said with confidence I would pin the bow. I had a trusted deck crew standing on the bow to call ranges ahead – this is normal, and on this yacht, due to the height of the bow, the water closer than 80 metres was obscured. To reduce radio chatter, I had an instruction passed for him just to use hand signals, with each finger representing a metre. I had good sight to him, and this would keep the radio clear for the bosun standing on the aft deck, calling distances for our stern clearance. This system was working well until he started to fumble with his fingers moving his thumb up and down: feeling the stress of the moment, I (a little too) abruptly asked the chief officer to find out what he was doing.

The chief officer called down on the radio, tersely asking the signals to be kept clear and not to mess around. The deckhand on the bow said he understood but he was trying to show the best hand gesture to indicate we were half a metre from the dock. As serious as this was, it gave a moment of levity to the proceedings and I said we would agree that a thumb represents half a metre, and it would be good if we don't have to use it again. There were some muffled giggles from the back of the bridge that I didn't acknowledge.

That was the zenith of the risk, and the yacht was now turning towards the exit and a safe heading: another 60 degrees of careful turn and we would be on our exit track.

Again, to keep a fig leaf over the absence of a true plan, I said to the bridge team confidently that we would continue to turn at 20 degrees rate of turn, steady on the exit course, which would be very close to due east, and then depart the port at a speed of 2–3 knots. When abeam of the end of Quai Rainier III, we would speed up to 4–5 knots to make a safe turn into the sea. This all happened according to the brief and the yacht continued with no further incident towards the anchorage at Saint-Jean-Cap-Ferrat, where the guests would rejoin after their dinner ashore. As the bosun reported from the transom that the yacht had cleared the port, the chief officer and I let out a schoolboy-like giggle, a release of nervous energy.

The chief officer finally broached the subject as we were on passage and it was only the two of us on the bridge. 'I know why you wanted to do that, but it was wrong and against all of what we teach and should practise.' I had nowhere to go, aside from acknowledging this criticism fully. I started with a weak defence, using my intimacy with the port and their radio approval, but gave this up as it was not valid and we both knew it. A peace descended on the bridge: we were colleagues and friends. The chief had said what needed to be said and I had acknowledged my chastisement. After a moment, I said in my most open and inviting tone, 'Hey, next time, talk me out of it, OK.' He smiled but let me know I didn't provide these openings and do not appreciate the interjection. This was the true rebuke to my behaviour; he was correct and by the force of my will I carried plans through with only the thinnest veneer of working within a team. There is little recourse to a bullish captain at sea: many of the normal checks and balances of business and life are not present. This is both an attraction of the role and a terrible risk.

Before I was allowed to dive deeper into my own thoughts, the chief engineer came to the bridge. The engineer was a ball of energy that, for the most part, he channelled for good. With a grin, he said, 'Well, we got through that one.' The chief officer and I nodded in unison; we both assumed he had observed the port through the cameras in the control room and was impressed with our execution. He hadn't and he wasn't. In my haste and tunnel vision towards the port entry, we had overlooked the simple action of draining the water in the 90-tonne swimming pool. It was standard practice and if I had allowed the time to follow the checklist it would have been done. The significance of this omission was that the water overflowed, cascading down two decks into the propulsion motor room.

As we were wondering just how to enter the port, the engineers were battling to keep the propulsion motor from being soaked from above. If they had failed, it would have resulted in loss of power to the starboard propeller and our ability to manoeuvre. They were aware of how constrained we were, how critical a power loss anywhere during the time would be, and they stayed focused on keeping the equipment running. As the chief was telling his story, it came to me again that I had created all this pressure. My commitment to delivering what should not have been possible has often been the secret to my success, but knowing when to draw the line is the real challenge. That evening in Monaco, there was a razor's edge between success and catastrophic failure that I shudder in retelling. The loss of a main propulsion motor at any time through the manoeuvre would have resulted in damage to our vessel at an absolute minimum. More likely, it would have resulted in a collision with one or more other yachts in the port, and that's putting aside the absolute embarrassment to the yacht owner that would have been without recompense.

The chief engineer left, still with a smile, and the thought of a 'near miss' was in the forefront of my thoughts as we approached the anchorage for the second time that day. We had the best of working relationships with the Port of Nice pilots and by the time they boarded we were only a few minutes from our final position. This could have caused tension, as technically we had entered the pilotage area without the pilot on board. I was ready for a telling-off from the pilot, but it must have shown on my face as he said, 'Captain, why don't I help the officer of the watch to the anchorage and you take a break.' 'Thank you, Pilot.' I continued to monitor the approach from the captain's chair but the combination of trust in the officer of the watch and respect for a professional French pilot left me to relax in my own thoughts: there would be at least two hours before the guests' return, when I would again have to return to a high focus.

The bubbly Swedish chief stewardess came to the bridge and after three hours of tension her presence was welcome.

She saw me slouched in the chair and with her characteristic Scandinavian candour said, 'Alright for some to lie back and relax!' Her irreverence caught the pilot off guard and I could see he did not appreciate this being directed to a fellow seafaring captain. 'It's OK, Pilot, she is under instruction from my wife to give me a hard time.' She continued, 'So, have you looked at any social media?' I hadn't, for the reason she knew: I do not have social media accounts. 'You're scoring well tonight, with 20,000 Instagram views.' I was not following fast enough, and then it dawned on me that every person on every yacht I saw in the port and every person in an apartment or restaurant facing the port was probably holding a phone and filming our manoeuvre. Of course they were going to post it as soon as possible.

'Thanks, I didn't know.' So after dealing with the maritime mirrors I held myself accountable to, I now needed to inform the management group that represented the yacht's owner that my actions had put the yacht in the 'trending' category of social media. For an industry that prides itself on privacy, this was the equivalent of 'that iceberg'. To their shared credit, and that of the yacht owner, they all appreciated the effort to provide the ultimate guest experience and no further action was taken.

From a distance, my actions may have looked like the yacht captain that I wanted to be, delivering the impossible yet again. Pulling the curtains back on the details behind the event, it can be seen as anything but. My recklessness snuck through without punishment on this occasion but, given time, the same attitude unchecked will only ever end in one horrible and inevitable outcome.

The story has a final, galling footnote. The next day, the yacht's mercurial agent from Monaco, a great friend of many years, rang: 'The port want to write some form of warning for your sunset stunt last night. Did you know the Prince was at the yacht club receiving guests when you stopped there?' I didn't know about the Prince and I flushed with some embarrassment as I recalled the group being photographed as we stopped. But as deserved as it was, I was not ready to take this admonishment. I pointed out that the details of the yacht had been passed twice to the port and that we had a record of the VHF radio transcript available if the port requested to listen. Several days later I received a follow-up message: 'All is good with the port, don't do it again.' 'Not in this lifetime!' An easy response.

Know your limitations

The temptation to please must be kept in check: know your limitations, know the limitations of those around you and know the limitations of your equipment.

Clients in all spheres are looking for the consistently amazing, not fame through misadventure.

I thought he was taller

When talking about our respective careers and useful insights we've gained through them, you might think my friends would ask me about business, personal success behaviours or anything I have observed with the guests that might benefit them, but no. The one thing my friends want to know about my life as a superyacht captain is: are the parties better? Well, yes and no. Yes, because the scope and scale are like nothing we could imagine. No, because so very little is left to chance. I like a party that evolves without a guiding hand, where drinks run out and friends misbehave and embarrass themselves. That said, I could be tempted... So, how does a billionaire throw a party?

Saint Barthélemy, always shortened to St Barths, is a small slice of France in the West Indies. The amount of the subsea former volcano that pierces the Caribbean Sea is only 25 square kilometres, but what a 25 it is. Geographically there is nothing to separate it from the other islands in the area, but it is so very different when the guests arrive for the Christmas and New Year holiday.

It was the dark hours of early morning when we anchored among the many boats jostling for prime position in front of Gustavia port. Distances are foreshortened in darkness and even though the radar screens were telling the truth and the yacht had sufficient room, I felt like we could reach and touch the other yachts in the anchorage. I took a last look at the radars, matched their information with what I could see and, knowing the weather forecast held no surprises, I departed for a couple of hours' sleep before the beginning of what I knew would be a long day: the first of several.

I awoke a few hours later to a glorious Caribbean day. The yachts that had concerned me so in the darkness now looked safely beyond arm's reach. My office was adjacent to the bridge and I moved between the two work areas throughout the day, each time checking with the officer of the watch to see if we could further optimise our location. I needed to keep their focus towards always shifting a little closer to the 'perfect' spot. The perfect spot is one that gives most shelter, shortens the guests' transfers in the tenders and, in a nod to my truth, makes me feel that I have done the best I can. I am very conscious that for all my efforts, mostly nobody else notices.

We had raised the anchor at sunrise and were sitting in dynamic positioning to hold the vessel in place. Dynamic positioning utilises position sensors, a computer model of the ship, its thrusters and the effects of wind and current to hold position or shift to a new location as ordered by the operator. As opportunity presented, we executed some responsible but challenging moves to relocate the yacht around other vessels like a 10,000-tonne draughts piece.

It was just before lunch break and I asked the bosun to come to the bridge. The bosun was an excellent crew member and understood yachting well. His instructions from me were to visit the purser, collect six envelopes with €500 in each, send a tender with one charming male crew member and one charming female to visit each of the six boats ahead of us and offer them the envelope to relocate for the next 36 hours.

In parallel to my playing yacht draughts, the day was busy. We were to host a party the next night, 30 December, for 250 guests. It was by invitation only, with security ashore and at the boarding area of the yacht. We needed RSVPs today so I could update the yacht's owner when I met him the next morning at St Maarten airport. Every few hours I checked in with the various department heads for a five-minute standing meeting for updates on any barriers to their achieving what was needed.

The tenders not encouraging the yachts in our sought-after anchorage to move were shuttling constantly, bringing aboard flowers, additional music equipment, ice for the ice bar and luge (flown in especially), speciality foods, dancers for the rehearsal and the Cuban lady for the hand-rolled cigar station. (When the cigar station was suggested to me it was an obvious yes, but as I watched the many bags of accessories being passed to the yacht, I had a moment's second thought. I never expected so much to be needed to create such a small item.)

Cigar installations aside, the day was progressing without incident; it was not our first party and we knew the formula for success. I indulged the security team, who had flown in from the owner's various residences to bolster numbers for the big event, with their request to give me a thorough briefing of all their actions. All the other teams were too busy actually working to sit down and have a meeting about their work, but personal security is a special group that needs nurturing when not lifting weights. Fortunately, the officer of the watch interrupted the briefing, just as I was at risk of drifting into a light nap as they explained their radio protocol. Our couple in the tender had woven their magic and five of the six yachts had moved completely and the sixth would move to the edge of our 'swinging circle' later, they did not wish to move further as one of their guests had been invited to our party. 'Let's move on in' was my response to the officer of the watch as I returned to the bridge. I told security we could reconvene later, hoping they would be kept busy by going to the gym or watching a Jason Bourne film. The day ended with all but the last items on board and the yacht anchored securely in the perfect location. I went out on deck for a couple of hours to work alongside the deck crew and enjoy their company. We could do a lot, but not fully prepare, as there were multiple helicopter flights in the morning, and the downdraughts from the rotors required everything to be packed away.

Early the next morning I boarded the first helicopter for the short flight to St Maarten to meet the yacht owner's private jet. I had a 90 per cent complete guest list with me and had checked the names several times to be ready for any questioning. There were no questions. The yacht owner, his partner and I were passengers in the first helicopter, and there were six further trips for each of the two helicopters to bring guests and their luggage to the yacht from the jet. The house band were in this group, as were some personal friends. The RSVP list read like a cross between the Oscars, a professional sports event and the Davos conference. If there was ever to be a gathering of the great and the good, tonight was it.

The weather stayed true to forecast with only light breezes and all was going well in the early afternoon. The live band were tuning the extended sound system, and two decks below the DJ was doing the same; the catering team was racking out hundreds of serves to go to the various stations, the deck teams were carrying the many large coolers of magnificent drinks, and of course the security team was seeking to check radio protocols. At these advanced stages of preparation there is no need for me to gather the department heads; they are busy and will let me know when they need my support. I walked around checking in on people, giving some praise and sharing a laugh. I did see areas to be improved but, more importantly, the crew knew someone appreciated their efforts.

Guests could arrive by their own tender or one of the yacht's, and from 7pm we were operating four boats concurrently, with each being capable of taking 14 guests. This simple process needed firm co-ordination to work and when at one point I observed, from the helicopter deck, more than ten tenders backed up, I asked the bosun to intervene. Within a few piercing whistles and confident, policeman-at-the-intersection-style arm movements, the tenders were moving in an efficient manner. I had indulged myself and added a personal friend to the guest list: he was a yacht broker, a group that normally would never be invited to an event like this. He had promised me, and I trusted him, that he would never cross the line and go into 'sales' mode. As he stepped on board from a tender the bosun had waved in, I welcomed him warmly, though with some nerves.

There was a receiving line, and it started with a magnetic wand security check and ID verification to confirm the person was on the guest list. I respected the necessity of this, but it went against my sense of billionaire style. Next was a refreshing towel served by a stewardess, a drink served by one of two stewards and then I was positioned to greet guests. It may sound twee, but guests like to see the captain, to know who is looking after their safety. The pace wasn't as fast as I'd have liked, but we found our rhythm of how to greet guests, make them feel special and move them on.

A known singer, a small fellow, was being demonstratively loud about being delayed by this process. In contrast, the Australian billionaire James Packer (a towering figure with a room-filling laugh) was just behind the rock star waiting to complete the boarding process when he heard my Australian accent and said to his group, 'Hey everyone, they have an Aussie skipper.' When he passed along the line to me, I apologised for the delay. He didn't care and shook my hand so strongly and was so authentic in his gratitude for the invitation that I felt proud to be Australian. I was also pleased that the retreating rock star saw this display of good grace and it made his small frame seem to diminish just a little more. In years since this evening in St Barths I have observed in various press this singer being a force for social good, maybe he was just having a bad night.

Within moments of this there was a kerfuffle at the security station on board, as the radio questioned if there was an additional guest list to the one held ashore (there wasn't). At the shoreside security point there was a guest, not on their list, loudly proclaiming she should be granted entry anyway; it seemed a young heiress was sure her name would be enough. The brush-cut moustached 60-year-old ex-US Marines helicopter pilot gave no recognition to her and gently barred her path to the tender: her party would have to wait until next year. This caused great merriment in the crew mess later when the pilot shared; he actually had never heard of the 'famous for being famous' young heiress. 'So what does she do?' was his only question. Fair question and it was left unanswered.

As the majority of guests had boarded, I moved through the yacht to see how the planning was holding up. I was stopped by the founder of an internet search company to explain some details of the submarine; the *Star Wars* founding family wanted to know if one of the younger children could sit in a helicopter; and a group of beautiful models were looking a little lost, so I escorted them to where the music was. There was a recording studio/sound stage and as I escorted my small group to the upper deck, I passed stars of stage, screen, business, music and sports. The models melted into the crowd and I was left alone to find a view of the stage. A Pink Floyd member was playing a guitar, Billy Joel was singing, members of the eighties band Duran Duran were filling some of the other spaces, and playing base guitar – very well, too – was the yacht owner. Maybe as I saw the yacht owner, perspiring, holding his own with some of the best musicians in the world, I humbly accepted: yes, along with being a genius and a visionary, he throws a great party.

The party continued. At some point it retreated from a mass gathering to a more intimate affair. Yachts have many private nooks, and several were in use with quiet conversations and some with a little more. Around four in the morning the butler/steward called me to say that the owner had withdrawn to his cabin for the night. This was my signal and I asked the crew to sweep through the yacht gently and let guests know that the last tenders were being arranged to take them to shore or to their yachts. It worked well with small groups, entwined pairs, some famous and some not, all being escorted to the back of the yacht. After the first main sweep it reduced to just a few and then a little bit longer and the very last guests gathered for their trip ashore. I did not stay on the swim platform for this process, preferring to retreat to the privacy of the bridge, and was advised over radio by the bosun when the very last guest had departed. He continued on the open radio channel that as the last guest had boarded, he had turned and said, 'Please tell the captain, Jonathon says thanks for the party.' My friend had achieved the unthinkable: he was the last guest to depart.

Parties and paparazzi

One reason yachts are so well suited to billionaire parties is that they are beyond the reach of the paparazzi. It is not reported or taken into account that the celebrity photo that is a triumph for the photographer is a failure for someone else, likely a personal staff member like me, trusted with the privacy of the guests...

The yacht had docked in Ibiza, and at over 100 metres it was a tight fit. The preferred practice was always to stay at anchor for the guests, but the weather forecast was terrible and with thoughts of Monaco and unplanned entries on my mind, it was the correct thing to do. The private plane landed, the transfer was by cars (not helicopter), the guests boarded the yacht and the yacht owner pulled me to the side to confirm, in person, his displeasure that the yacht was in port. We had exchanged messages for the past 24 hours, but I knew he would want to chastise again my poor management of the weather. I took the telling-off for what it was but did not dwell. I had hoped to leave almost immediately after their arrival as the winds had eased; however, the port had responsibly put a very low wind limit on movements after an incident the previous year, so we were bound to remain.

There was a concert in the evening at the Ushuaïa Club by the resident DJ, David Guetta. We had secured a private area for our guests for a fee that in my personal life would have paid for a new car. I cannot see the attraction of one man and a couple of turntables but given the size of the event my judgement is best discounted.

With the chance to move to anchor removed and after dining on board, the guest group left the yacht for the club in a fleet of vehicles. There was another little hiccup as the cars could not stop directly at the foot of the yacht's boarding gangway – the walk was only 70 metres but the yacht owning couple again shared their displeasure that I had not been able to improve this to their standards. These rebukes are common and I, like all my colleagues, just wear them and keep moving. Perfection is a terrible taskmaster.

As luck would have it, the weather eased, and we departed Ibiza dock early the next morning. A further two days into the trip, one of the guest's personal assistants paid an early visit to the bridge. The personal assistants are often more work than their guests, especially those from the US, who seem to have a total geographic blindness for anything beyond their borders. On this morning, the PA was in a total flap: that walk to the cars at the dock had given the paparazzi the chance to photograph the guests, who included a Grammy-Award-winning singer and a world-famous supermodel.

There was nothing I could have done to avoid the occurrence at the time or now put the genie back in the bottle. When the PA said how upset the guests would be, I said, 'I cannot own their emotions, and I cannot control the actions of others.' My statement was to reaffirm this to myself, as the yacht's owner held me entirely accountable and we had a strained relationship for the remainder of this trip. Moving forward, the conversation of 'paparazzi-safe locations' was always in the trip planning.

I have grown stronger in taking full ownership for events that are within my control. In parallel, I am more aware of what is not in my control and the importance of not allowing this to own my emotions.

More than weather, more than paparazzi, what is not in my control is the response and behaviours of others.

I am still learning to live this lesson.

Everything has a purpose

There are no accidents in the world of billionaires. The parties, the film festivals, the Grand Prix races are all for a purpose. When billionaires meet, it is for their solar systems of knowledge, information and access to intertwine and grow. It is implicit in every interaction that their sharing of information will benefit both parties; it is an obsession with billionaires to do favours for each other. A referral, an introduction, an insight – it all matters. Sometimes these favours benefit the billionaire; sometimes they have a wider positive impact. The superyacht is the ultimate platform for this exchange and as the captain I am intensely aware that the yacht commands a central place on the billionaire's stage. When I see the guest list, I am aware, even if not all names are familiar, that all have been chosen for a purpose. I take a deep pride in the very small part that I and the crew play as the facilitators of these relationships.

I had been working as captain for a 'still active in business' yacht owner for two years. The importance of his working status is that the yacht was not recreational: it was a strategic business asset. The weekly changing guests were curated; incredibly so. The yacht moved around the world to match holidays in various cultures. The guests were brought on as families and the itineraries for the trips were pored over and deconstructed down to their value components by the yacht owner. This approach had continued for some time and it became our operating profile. The schedule was so tight that there was one occasion when the first tender was departing with one guest group as the second tender was bringing the new guests in. We shifted our entire operating focus to match the new guests and we did it in minutes. A few weeks after this the routine had not slowed, and during a glorious summer's day in the Southern Central Mediterranean, we were entertaining multiple families from multiple yachts. This was a group I and the crew knew well; they had all visited before and there was an intimacy to the day. (I say 'intimacy' within the framework that the lines never blurred: crew were staff and guests were to be treated with a respect beyond question.)

Even in this warm environment, I remained true to my own boundaries and when a guest asked the cost of the yacht and its operating budget, I declined to answer. In a light but firm tone, I cited my respect for the privacy of my employer. In response, I received a warm hand on my shoulder and a knowing 'of course'. A couple of hours passed until I returned to where the guests, all fellow billionaires, and their families were gathered. The same guest once again sought my ear. This time, as he approached he thumbed over his shoulder towards the yacht's owner, and said, 'It's OK – you can tell me everything.' I too looked to the yacht owner and received a subtle nod in confirmation. 'Well, if that is the case, here it is. The yacht cost around €250 million at purchase and the operation costs around €13 million per year.' The guest nodded, and while looking over the side of the yacht to his children playing said, 'It makes sense. One deal secured on board will pay it all back many times over, and it is pretty hard to say no after your kids have been hosted so well for a week.' That moment, all the pieces joined together. The yacht, the extravagance and the care taken in curating these family holidays were just side plays on a bigger board.

There is nothing menacing, illegal or immoral about this. It is as normal for a billionaire to seek to leverage through every interaction as two neighbours on any suburban street talking about the property market, the local schools or where is the best value for servicing their cars. It also speaks to the scale of their lives that the yacht is a mere trinket to the greater operation.

There is one group that recognises the power of these interactions and removes the element of chance by arranging a four-day retreat at which the greatest wealth, the greatest minds and the generally interesting can spend time together. This annual gathering is held via a seriously curated invitation list and, while held in beautiful seclusion, it is not about decadence.

The camp has received some negative environmentally focused press owing to the number of private jets and private helicopters involved in moving the guests to and from their coastal Mediterranean retreats. Having arrived by (motor) yacht, we too could have fallen prey to the same criticisms. It played on my mind as we hosted tech founders, venture capitalists, sports heroes and stars of the screen. With the world facing down a yet to be fully understood environmental crisis, how could this be justified? I would like to suggest to the 'other eight billion' global citizens not attending, that the travel, the consumption, the camp in its entirety *was* justified for this elite group. These people are the thinkers, the funders, those that inspire and the spokespeople who will combine to find a healthy future for our communities and our planet.

This is not a sycophantic crush on this global elite – not all billionaires will sit in this category. Some I have worked for use their means largely for their own benefit. They are closer to modern tzars, Roman emperors or the court of Louis XIV; their solar systems are not built to find solutions to global crises, but to indulge their every desire. Those at the retreat are a far smaller group, who wish their legacy to be something greater, something that will outlive even their global business creations.

We spent four days anchored by the event. The yacht worked long days and evenings moving guests from shore to yacht, providing the platform for conversations, for abstract thinking and for new relationships to be developed. My personal impact in the history of humanity may be slight, but for these few days I felt like an enabler to those who may be the saviours in a future that will need some heroes and heroines.

Enabling has its own rewards

There is merit and personal peace to be found in accepting that there are some great minds in our global community whose insights we need for our shared future.

We need to be bigger than our daily judgements and allow them the room to reach their greatness.

Fantasy staff game

Desires enabled by a limitless budget can boggle the imagination. They are diverse and undertaken concurrently: there are the parties, the philanthropic endeavours, the art collection, the asset management, the travel, and the constant goal of further expanding already expansive business empires. Like the nation states the billionaires resemble, managing these many spinning wheels needs people – lots of people. Estates need gardeners (many), kitchens need chefs, helicopters need pilots, polo teams need horse trainers, and parties need all sorts of characters. It doesn't stop with the easily observed: finance teams, legal, counselling, coaches... it does not end.

I often play a game with friends not exposed to the yachting community or the billionaires underwriting it. I invite them to let their imagination run wild and think of a life where their staff take care of everything, and I really mean everything. I push them to think through what roles they would like filled, and to realise their every need could be taken care of by a specialised staff member. Not one overworked housekeeper, but a team of specialists. I draw on my experience with the yacht owners I have spent decades working for, and how they have their needs met by a staff that extends into the hundreds.

I know hundreds seems quite ridiculous, and I remember my first awakening to this when I was given an internal telephone directory for one of the families I worked for. I flipped through the pages with a grin of incredulity. I felt the need to ring each number to prove the person existed; I saved myself the embarrassment and over time I met most, and they were all real. The sample below roughly reflects this directory.

Primary home staff (chefs, housekeepers, groundsmen, service staff)	22
Secondary home staff	8
Tertiary home staff	4
Ranch	10
Vineyard	10
Office staff	14
	68

Aviation	
Fixed-wing pilots	12
Stewardess (air)	4
Helicopter	8
Mechanic (air)	6
Admin (air)	2
	32

Personal finance and legal	
Various titles	20
HR (manage staff)	2
	22

Admin	
PAs	4
EAs	4
Events	2
Art	2
	12
Personal	
Trainer	2
Beautician	2
Drivers	4
Security	12
Medical	4
Nanny/tutors	6
	30
Yacht(s)	
Crew and support	130
	130
Total	294

Since that time, I have worked for another yacht-owning family whose personal staff were double this and I know there are larger again. I think this average number is enough to make the point.

I have already mentioned my disappointment in the Bond franchise for short-changing their villains with assets and personal staff, and I have not even considered henchmen or laser-guided shark trainers. Bond villains aside, the fantasy staff game's theme is that it must be wonderful to have all of your needs met by someone just waiting for you to ask for their help. I also tell my friends not to worry about staff salaries; in this game, your wealth is such that it is not even a consideration. Do you want to play?

It was a pleasant day and the yacht-owning family, with their guests, had stepped ashore for the morning. Traditionally, they were not early risers and it surprised me that the group had made it off the yacht en masse in such good time. When guests depart a yacht, the names are always called to the bridge by crew radio. I was visiting the bridge at the time and as I observed the officer of the watch take note of the names, I noticed that one of the children was not with the main group. I asked the chief stewardess by the internal phone if this was correct and she said the owners' youngest child had remained on board as she was unwell and taking a course of antibiotics that the crew nurse was in charge of.

Following this news, I called for the nurse, to check she also knew – I do trust the information I am given by my team, but I tend to follow the Reagan-era maxim of 'Trust, but Verify'. The nurse confirmed the young guest had an infection: it was minor, but the parents had asked for a broad-spectrum prescription of antibiotics. The nurses on board the yachts are all registered in their home countries and follow tight protocols. Before any prescription-level medications are given, the nurse calls the medical service ashore and gains the approval of the doctor. It is a belt and braces approach. The tight following of protocols is an important backstop when reporting on all crew and guests, but especially the case when it is the yacht-owning family's child. I also never forget and remind the nurses often that while they are the medical professionals, the captain remains the person responsible for all medical treatment. This does not diminish their greater knowledge and training but is a reflection on the maritime environment where the captain is the legally responsible person for all events.

Both due to my responsibility and to ensure I was fully informed, I asked the dose, frequency and duration of the antibiotics. In my personal life I am not so quick to seek antibiotics and wanted to know how long an 11-year-old child was receiving the prescription. It was the second day, and the next dose was due at 10.30, one hour from our call. I rang off and didn't think much more about it; the nurse had worked with the yacht for a year and was well liked by all guests. From my perspective, she was a well-regarded crew member, and I always sought her counsel on medical issues. I returned to my office and at 11.30 heard on the radio that the main guest party were returning to the yacht by tender. I made my way to the transom to greet them. I do not always do this, but when it is the yacht owners returning, I make sure I am visible in case they wish to give any guidance or ask questions. On this occasion, the nurse was also there with the – clearly unwell – young child.

The wife of the yacht owner swept on board and brushed past me to see her daughter; she was a caring mother but chose the timing of her maternal instincts to suit her social life. Her first question to her daughter that I could overhear was, 'Did the nurse give you your medication on time?' I thought it a little off-key with the nurse standing not more than 3 metres away and clearly waiting to give a report on the girl's health. I turned my primary focus from the wife to the husband, who was at the same time ascending the stairs from the swim platform. He was a couple of steps from joining me when we heard a scream from his wife: 'Who do you think you are? You are not a nurse, you are an embarrassment!' The yacht owner and I again looked at each other: though his eyes had narrowed, it was (if I read it correctly) a combination of concern for his daughter and a caution to me lest the outburst be valid.

The owner and I were not going to find out as his wife left the aft deck at pace, with their daughter following. The husband, who was incredibly polite and conscious of maintaining decorum in every interaction, excused himself and followed his wife and daughter. The other guests, equally aware of the shift in mood, skirted past without eye contact and slipped quietly into the guest accommodation.

From standing on a very full aft deck just two minutes earlier, I was now alone – at least, I thought I was. The nurse stepped out from behind a pillar, sobbing uncontrollably. I moved towards her, both to console and to understand what had just caused the outburst. Through her sobs, she said that the daughter innocently answered her mother's question that the medication had been given at 10:45, a full

15 minutes past the prescribed time. She had apologised and explained that it had taken 15 minutes to find the girl, who had gone to her absent friend's cabin to play on their computer. It was as far as she had gone with the explanation before the outburst from the mother cut her story short and silenced all in earshot. I did a physical double-take and rhetorically asked, 'What? Does 15 minutes even matter?' I knew the answer, but I also knew that this incident had not ended. I directed the nurse to call the doctor and gain in writing that a 15-minute delay in taking a broad-spectrum antibiotic did not matter. She wrote, and the doctor replied: it did not matter in the slightest.

I was in the captain's office two hours later when the yacht owner knocked on the open door and entered. I could never fault his courtesy to me, to the crew and to everyone I saw him engage with. Even when it was to scold, he was faultlessly polite. He was an embodiment of all the good that can be gained from generational wealth and elite education. I stepped around from my desk to greet him, conscious to embed some added formality and humility. I then sat in the office chair adjacent to where he had sat down. I waited. English was not this yacht owner's first language, and he was very conscious of his wording and phrasing; it was endearing in many ways, and it gave for a melodic tone to his dialogue. 'Brendan, this nurse is not very good.' We were not off to the best start and I knew better than to contradict. 'She missed my daughter's medication and upset my wife, what should we do?'

There it is, the poison question. What I wanted to say was, what we should do is get over this and move on. What I actually said was, 'What would you like to happen?' The yacht owner, continuing the theme of courteousness, said, 'She can stay for this trip but at the end you should let her go, making sure she is paid everything in her contract.' There was only one response due of me: 'Yes, of course.' He excused himself and left.

The tale of the medication is one of the few truly disappointing events in a varied career. It sat with me because the delay was not the nurse's fault and in any case it did not matter. It was so truly a case of wielding power for power's sake. But unlike this experience, there have been many other 'delegation fails' that I have lived through and come out smiling on the other side.

I found the Cannes Film Festival red-carpet tickets in the 'non-chosen' clutch bag of the yacht owner's wife. I say 'non-chosen' as there was a choice of three equally valid bags placed on the seat in the tender by the assistant for Madame to choose from, a shell game for the tickets if you will. They were still on the seat as, in company with her best friend, the yacht owner's wife was terribly late for the red-carpet premier and had left them behind. The premier followed a whirlwind of jet-skiing, champagne in the Jacuzzi, an extended period in the spa and finally make-up and hair. The assistant, in a last-ditch effort to support her employer, put the bags in the tender with a strong logic of 'She has to get in the smaller boat to depart the yacht'.

The tickets were placed half in, half out, again to reinforce which of the three bags they were in. Really, the assistant had made it foolproof. Hold that thought.

Madame failed the shell game with the tickets still clearly visible in the unchosen bag that remained in the tender. Yes, it was a failure on our part, and I felt a weight of disappointment as I sent crew running through the concourse of Cannes trying to locate the two guests and hand the tickets over. Against my requests, the women had not allowed security to accompany them and we were blind to their movements. Madame did accept my business card for a number to text if she needed anything, but I did not hold her temporary French phone number.

The two were not found and there was a period of nervousness as we expected some 'blowback' from the mistake. It didn't happen; the two women returned four hours later, a little drunk and laughing after being turned away from the film, which they didn't really wish to see anyway. As they were trying to negotiate their ticketless entry, they were recognised and invited to the highly sought-after private party of Elton John. The quaking assistant was standing beside me and received an authentic hug from Madame, who said through giggles, 'It was my fault, I was late... but we had more fun anyway.' I let out a visible sigh of relief and Madame noticed and said, 'Look at the poor captain, always worrying about something.' She was right, I always worry when my guests are in motion and out of my sight.

I have always enjoyed the relationship with the personal staff of the yacht-owning families, from personal assistants to art curators to personal shoppers. The strongest ties have always been with the helicopter and fixed-wing pilots: there is a kinship between us as operators in shared worlds of maritime and aviation. I had a particularly strong relationship with a Swiss-Italian pilot who had worked with the yacht owner for a long time. He was a source of intelligence like no other and helped me on many occasions. As a protocol, he would always call on take-off from Switzerland to assist my time planning for his arrival.

On this particular yacht, the importance of the call was both to allow the yacht to depart from port on time to receive the helicopter… and also to advise the yacht crew whether the helicopter was travelling with or without the pet dog. The Pomeranian lapdog was critical, not due to any animal health customs declaration (which was the story we had built around the call for the guests' benefit), but because it was an indicator of who was in the helicopter. The dog's owner and constant companion was the wife of the yacht owner. If the dog was in the helicopter, so was she. If no dog was in the helicopter, so was somebody else.

On this day, I took the phone call and repeated immediately after on the yacht's internal radio, 'Helicopter launched, no dog, I repeat no dog today.' That radio call caused a wave of activity. When no dog was travelling, the interior team had to change the yacht from being ready for the wife to being ready for the mistress. The dresses in the master cabin, the family photos on the side cabinets, the bathroom supplies, the drinks list, the menus and so much more – all had to be exchanged. The helicopter flight was one and a half hours, so the team had to move fast to make the changes and then be ready to greet the guest party. We, along with the husband, the wife and the mistress, all knew that all knew. The arrangement had been in place for decades, well before my idea of arranging the call with the helicopter pilot, but nevertheless the fig leaf was essential for social respectability.

The helicopter landed. The chief stewardess stood by the passenger door ready to assist the passengers. We had trained her to be one of the helicopter landing assistants as she was the most recognised and trusted by the guests. I would stand in front of the helicopter to watch everything and be ready to welcome guests as they entered the reception area. The rotors slowed and the chief stewardess continued to wait beside the sliding door to ensure no passenger left the airframe before the rotors were absolutely stopped. This is about a two-minute process and somewhere through this she turned to me with eyes wide and a stricken look on her face. The Pomeranian was eagerly jumping from the lap of the owner's wife towards the door.

The guests disembarked and the chief stewardess greeted them and smiled: they walked to me and I greeted them and smiled. Neither of us could use our radios to call the interior crew so they could move at least some of the most visible items. What the chief stewardess and I did not know was that the bridge officer had seen the dog on the camera and made the emergency call. In the time it took the guests to move from the helicopter to their cabin a lot had been achieved, to the point where to the non-practised eye it looked correct. Unfortunately, the owner's wife had a very practised eye and noticed the small things. We hadn't pulled off the save of the decade. The yacht owner called me to his cabin after he and his guests had dined. His wife had adjourned to the spa. 'Brendan, I hope you never have such a situation, but if you do I recommend making sure the correct dresses are hanging when your wife comes into your room. Please don't make the same mistake again.' He laughed, I laughed, and I wished I was somewhere else.

Another boat, another year. My yacht owner had tripped on a raised wooden plank on the dock. He cursed the port, cursed the French and returned to the yacht livid and in some pain. It was before the days of on-board registered nurses and he called me to inspect the finger he had hurt in the fall. It looked painful and for sure it was dislocated. I showed him my own damaged hands from youthful endeavours of Australian Rules Football and assured him I knew the best action. I reset his finger, provided mild painkillers, placed two pieces of tape on his hand and the stewardess provided an ice pack.

The owner accepted me as the medic for his guests, but this was the first time I had given him any direct treatment. At the end of what was in all an eight-minute process, and as I was preparing to leave the room, the owner asked with some incredulity, 'Do you really know what you are doing? Get the helicopter ready!' It was again one of those many times when 'yes, of course' was the simplest response. The helicopter could make it to his home from the yacht without refuelling and my yacht owner had his cardiac surgeon standing by his private helipad to meet him on arrival. After departure, I did not hear any more from the pilots until after landing, when they confirmed they would spend the night and return early in the morning. Thinking of the consultant surgeon's assessment of my treatment did not impact my sleep and the next morning I was again standing in the reception area on the helideck to receive the returning helicopter.

As the yacht owner and his wife disembarked, my eye of course was drawn to his hand, and I noted there was new tape on the finger but identically placed to my own. To his absolute credit, the dismissive yacht owner of 12 hours earlier said, 'My surgeon said you took the correct actions, thank you.' I nodded, withheld my self-serving grin, and summer continued.

I will never have personal staff into the hundreds. I have two daughters, who, really, I work for, so that does not count either. I do, however, delegate responsibility many times in the day. The small interactions I am consciously outsourcing that I could potentially take responsibility for. I am trading time for payment and the promise of added skill. My bearing witness to the added complexity and angst that being personal staff brings makes me much more aware that regardless of the relationship and perceived/ advertised skill, the outcome remains my responsibility for having made the choice to engage the person in the first instance.

I have learned that owning your situations will give more happiness than 500 staff but, if pressed, maybe I would take the personal shopper and driver.

A challenge to a quiet life

The goal of my 'fantasy personal staff' game is to show that access to a person who will cater to your every wish may not be all it presents to be.

I seed the game with examples to serve my purpose, though with absolute certainty. Adding more complexity to your life through staff, assets to manage and increasing the number of engagements challenges the chance for a life where peace and contemplation are at the forefront.

Waitlessness

One of my favourite yacht-owning billionaires was having a golf lesson in New Zealand. He was a truly charming man and very approachable, and this was confirmed as the golf pro later relayed their conversation. The native New Zealand golf pro was trying to gauge the pace of the lesson and asked, 'What time is your flight?' The billionaire replied, 'When we finish.'

The pro was not following, and his face must have shown this. The billionaire continued, 'The plane and crew are already waiting, a helicopter is standing at the clubhouse for the transfer from the course to the airport and we will leave when the lesson is finished.' This is nothing too out of the ordinary, of course, in billionaire land, where planes and helicopters are used like family cars. The flight was from New Zealand to Europe and the yacht owner had bought a larger plane, specifically to undertake this journey as fast as possible: golf lesson or not, time matters.

Another yacht owner I spent a significant time with would respond to every piece of information with 'How long? Are you sure? Have you checked?' The quality of any experience would be determined by the efficiency of its execution. My aspiration as his captain was to create the most memorable impact in the shortest, most clearly defined and time-efficient period. Any transport had to be as direct as possible, the time for transfer from yacht to tender, tender to port, port to destination: all had to be checked and pre-driven. To unpack that set of measurements, prior to the yacht owner arriving, all possible anchorages for the yacht would be checked and the tenders that would take the guests to shore would test-drive the route to the port. Online maps are not good enough as there are often boat speed restrictions, or the port is busy and there are delays on entry. On arrival at the port, the crew would look to find the perfect dock – not too high and not too low – and then walk to where the cars would naturally park. Even this walk was timed and should never be further than 100 metres. The drivers also had to drive various routes to the airport to ensure the one chosen on the day was optimal. Luggage always travelled separately as the loading and unloading risked delaying the operation. Often there was a helicopter transfer option that also had to be investigated: where could the helicopter land in relation to the jet? Was there buggy transfer between the two? Could customs clearance occur in the plane or did the guests need to go into the terminal? I need to stop there, as the logistics for these arrivals and departures was almost infinite...

I would send all the timings to the yacht owner, who would then measure my performance by comparing the advised time with the actual time it took to move from the jet to the yacht. On one occasion, in a Pacific coastal community, there was a 'non-researched' pop-up street market that forced a detour. The market had not been in place during the reconnaissance drives and it had caused a variance to the advised transfer time. I would like to think I did not show it, but I was an anxious mess by the time the yacht owner arrived. His sideways glance was enough to assure me my failure had not gone unnoticed.

During the holiday, the time monitoring would continue. The definition of a successful event was to have no more than 30 minutes of transfer time, one hour at the destination and a corresponding 30-minute return transfer. This two-hour target was applied to all events, from a restaurant booking in Italy to touring ancient ruins in Greece or viewing polar bears in Svalbard, Norway. I was never able to communicate this imperative to the polar bears, who apparently maintained their own schedule: again, room for improvement in my performance.

This is not atypical. The billionaire yacht owners use every moment. They are extremely aware of the value of their time and will not wait idly for anything. If I were to tell you the most consistent way to upset a billionaire (and I think I have tried a few), it would be to make them wait... for anything! A term I like to use in describing the yacht guest experience is '*waitlessness*', a state where everything happens to your schedule. I recall a comment from a yacht owner who, after a laborious meeting with a shipyard management team, said: 'These guys do not value their own time so how can they value mine? I will not work with them any more.' There was no way back from this: we walked; the project ended.

I do not place my own interpretation of time onto others. Whether it is the eternally late Russian oligarch or the mechanically punctual Swiss industrialist, I respect their approach to time. If it is the former then I expect to wait, and I ensure I am not idle as I too respect my time. I do not stopwatch my life, but I am respectful of my own time and those of others I work or socialise with; whether it is a phone call or a meeting with colleagues, I have developed the courtesy of asking them how long they are available for. If I have 15 minutes to spare, I do not waste it: I can read, complete a task or sit peacefully and savour the moment. I would like to think that, as a result of these observations, I have found a balance between using my time wisely but (mostly) without the obsessiveness of billionaires.

I see a direct correlation between this time obsession and any professional conversation with the yacht-owning billionaires of my experience. With their hundreds of staff, companies across continents, and too many business structures to realistically remember, the billionaires could be excused for seeming distracted in conversation. This is not the case. With a consistency of 100 per cent, the yacht owners give their full attention to the conversation they are engaged in. All superyacht captains know that any time given to them by their employing yacht owner is precious; it requires deep preparation and will be ended abruptly if the quality of content dips below what the billionaire finds acceptable. Within this privileged time, the billionaires are piercing, inquisitive and do not allow the conversation to meander.

Like any of the positive observations, I have tried to emulate this level of focus, though possibly in a gentler way. Sadly, I usually fail with my attempts, with family, colleagues and all encounters. My goal is to make it a reflexive nature to be absolutely engaged with the person to whom I am speaking. I try not to glance at my watch, my phone or to the window, or to acknowledge passers-by in a social environment; a conversation is a shared moment of intimacy with another, and my goal is to give myself over to it completely. If all time is precious, then shared time in conversation is doubly so. I am a work in progress to delivering on this goal, but I continue to practise.

Invest in time

Time is the only investment you cannot recover once lost. Respect your own time, respect the time of others, and use both wisely.

Time is the one measure of wealth where you can overtake the billionaires: time at peace with yourself, time with the people you love and time at ease with your surroundings represents the ultimate luxury.

The illusion of normalcy

Clearly, the lives of the billionaires are very different and some of the examples stretch credulity, but what if that was your normal?

After the heady discussions on fantasy staff, it is worth coming back to a more normal space, but what is that? If everyone's normal is their own, then this is as much the same for the billionaire yacht owner as it is for all of us. Never was the normal-is-normal situation brought home to me more than when a young yacht-owning heiress was discussing with me her own normality in the context of being raised as a well-adjusted teenage girl. She was at pains to point out that she had experienced the joys and suffered the same challenges as all teenagers.

She, her elder sister and her younger brother fought, were chided by their parents and wanted to 'hang out' with their friends. At the time of our conversations, the iPhone generation was only just beginning, and she had been told to wait before she was given such a symbol of teenage social empowerment. I had heard this story multiple times and, in her defence, I think that they were as 'normal' as any family of yacht-owning billionaires I had encountered. The parents worked hard to ensure the third generation of wealth would continue their dynastic legacy with a sense of balance and social awareness.

We were standing together as the young heiress was waiting for her siblings to join her. They had all been invited to a friend's birthday. I had heard there was some arguing between the sisters about who was wearing what and the brother (the youngest) did not want to go to the party at all. So far, it is all very normal. Where the reference to a recognisable normality ended was the setting. We were standing on the aft deck of her family's 75-metre yacht and anchored adjacent to the private port/resort of her friend, the birthday child. Also anchored in the area were four other yachts of similar size, with other children waiting to be taken to the birthday party.

On cue, as I was about to respond with my own view of 'normal', a twin-engine private helicopter flew overhead, delivering more children to the birthday party. It was enough for me to mention to her that during my childhood I never attended a birthday party on a private estate, where friends arrived by yacht and private helicopter. She said, with some wonderful insight and with no malice or indignation, 'Well, that was your Normal and this is Mine.'

I reflected at the time and have many times since applied her wisdom to my own life. What makes any of our normal any more correct than the young heiress?

I sought to apply this fleeting conversation to my life and while it may seem completely self-evident, it began to give me a far greater understanding of the behaviour of others and I developed stronger empathy for their situations. I reside in a country where I am a non-native speaker and have the rare luxury as a tertiary-educated, white, English-speaking male of being a minority with communication limitations. My normal has changed and I can now view a different normal than, by luck alone, being born into privilege. Of course, my privilege does not extend to helicopters and yachts for my daughters' birthdays, but I remain eternally grateful for that little bit of wisdom shared on the back of a wonderful yacht.

Beware of projecting

It is natural to project our own situations onto others, but we must be aware that all of our perspectives are shaped by our experiences.

All our normals are ours alone.

Saint-Tropez sunset

It was late afternoon in Saint-Tropez, where the light is golden, and the people match the light. I was enjoying the spectacle and was relaxed walking alongside my yacht owner. Our relationship was relatively formal, though at times we – well, he – spoke freely.

'You know why this place is so crowded, Brendan?' He did not wait for my reply. 'It is because the many come to see the few like me. The few like me come to see each other and measure where we stand against each other.'

What a crazy, though insightful, thing to say. I would never think of visiting Saint-Tropez to ogle at wealth or measure where I sat in some imagined pecking order – or was I doing this without even being aware of it? Was this behaviour adding to everyone's pleasure or was this an example of 'Status Anxiety'? Alain de Botton's wonderful book of the same name develops the idea that, for each of us, our normal is defined by our own situation and that of our peer group. It is only through recognising and accepting this that we can find peace within ourselves.

When I was a navy cadet under training, I had minimal assets and even less cash; my friends had very little too, yet we were all having the time of our lives. There was the occasional aberration where someone had received a car from generous parents or had access to a holiday home, though unless they made these available to the wider group these assets were credited little social value. As time and careers moved forward (or not), the smallest of differences were identified and measured. The first person to buy their own home, the first to gain a directorship or open their own business, and so it continues. Among my group we have now come full circle; we have reached the age where we have landed where we are going to land and the competition has reduced: we are no longer cadets, but we are at peace again. I publicly and proudly say that I live my own life and do not try to 'keep up with the Joneses'. Is this the truth? Maybe I am still a little irritated when I learn that a less popular classmate has ascended the material ladder with more dexterity than I have. I know I bristle when I hear of a yacht captain starting out on a great yacht who (in my view only) will not carry the weight of their responsibility, nor work as hard or care as much as I would have done with the same opportunity. How can I know enough to make such judgements? Do I honestly care that the captain won't deliver for the owner? More likely it is my petty jealousy; it would be simpler to acknowledge they are at the very least my peer.

Luckily, when viewing yacht owners, I don't feel the same need for ranking. It is like envying a giraffe for being able to reach up higher on the tree to take leaves: the yacht owners' lives are so different to mine I have no reference to compare. What I do see is that while I cannot compare myself to a yacht owner, they certainly compare themselves with each other.

Cala di Volpe (Bay of the Fox) is in Sardinia. More precisely, it is in the heart of the Costa Smeralda, the north-east quarter of the otherwise humble Italian island that the visionary Aga Khan transformed into one of the great havens for the world's wealth. It is not uncommon to see 50 yachts all greater than 70 metres (€100 million each) anchored in the bay over the summer. Within that group there are likely to be five yachts above 100 metres, with values in excess of €200 million. The onshore villas are tasteful, worthy of the yachts and are also valued in the tens of millions.

On one of the beautiful summer afternoons in Cala di Volpe, my employer asked me to take him on a tour of the yachts in the bay. He was an experienced yacht owner, and I thought the purpose of the tour was to admire these modern wonders of design and engineering. As the tour continued, the yacht owner became increasingly agitated. As we passed each yacht, he would ask me for the details. I would respond with the 'weights and measures' of the yacht in question. My dialogue followed an objective framework: 'Yes, this yacht is 90 metres long, it was launched last year and is owned by an American tech mogul. The one behind is 120 metres long and was built for a Russian fellow with interest in minerals.' My own professional knowledge was enough to fill in the gaps at this level: this is the world I inhabit, and I can recite the details as a sports fan can speak of the performance of their favourite players.

'Take me back to my yacht, please' Unexpectedly, my employer lost interest and asked to return. A few minutes of silence passed between us until he shared: 'There was a time when my yacht [60 metres] was the most beautiful in the bay. How do I keep up with this new money?' I took that to be rhetorical and the silence continued.

I had wondered if status anxiety ended at a certain point of wealth: it doesn't! I learned on that afternoon in Cala di Volpe that, regardless of the happiness industry telling me that there is a certain balance of house, yoga, linen clothing and organic produce that will provide long-lasting inner peace, this is just not the case, and my yacht owner showed me that even with his immense wealth he was still comparing himself to his peers and feeling dissatisfied. This is biological and sociological. I learned to acknowledge the feeling, not worry about denying the sense of competition and not allow the emotion to result in bitterness. I do OK with this now, thanks to my yacht owner, and if it does cross my consciousness. I acknowledge the feeling and move on.

Competition

My observations of billionaires showed me there is no upper limit to competitive restlessness. This taught me that competition with others can even be healthy. It is the spark that pushes us to our own greatness – whatever that greatness looks like.

Embracing that this comes from somewhere deep inside my human operating system frees me to mock myself and in parallel harness the positive energy.

I am not trapped in feelings of insecurity when I see others outrunning me on the athletic track of life.

Bubbles and troubles

'There are bubbles coming from your buoyancy compensator! You can't leave the surface! Do you know how many people rely on you?'

We were about to dive the Poor Knights, New Zealand, one of the world's greatest dive locations, and the yacht owner was receiving the warning from one of his entourage.

I grew up in and around scuba and it is the most natural thing for me to take a group diving. Sometimes equipment has slow leaks, but it is not a problem – mostly it is air escaping from the folds and pockets where it is trapped. I acknowledged the comment from the well-meaning, though poorly informed, friend of the yacht owner and continued preparing the group to leave the surface for their dive. My motivation: once we'd left the surface, they could no longer talk.

The yacht owner at the centre of the concern was self-made, an active man by all standards. He played basketball, raced yachts at the highest level and generally lived an active and healthy lifestyle. The entourage for the morning dive were old friends, the kind of friends that 'knew him back when', and while they enjoyed the lifestyle of their anointed friend, they never let him forget his value to the wider community or bowed to his greatness.

Seeking, as always, to deliver beyond expectations, I had to move quickly through my annoyance at their overreaction and acknowledge their concern as their truth. I stopped the dive and reconfigured equipment. It was only a few minutes' delay, but it was enough for the yacht owner to change his mind, and he asked to return to his yacht. I was professional enough not to behave sullenly, but I felt that I had failed to execute the experience for my yacht owner and his guests, and my body language must have given enough clues to my disappointment. The yacht owner called me to sit with him in the small boat taking us back to the yacht. In a supportive schoolmasterly tone, he said, 'You think you let me down by stopping the dive.' I did and I nodded. 'You also think that my friend overreacted about the bubbles coming out of my buoyancy compensator.' This time I smiled a conspiratorial grin and nodded again.

The yacht owner then explained that he also knew the bubbles meant nothing and he felt safe with me in any case. We had spent significant time together over the past year and this confirmation was appreciated. He said his friends needed purpose now that his success was so extreme, and he was happy to indulge them (and more than that, he was hungry and did not need to dive today). He continued to reflect, with what I felt was truthfulness, on the life his success had chosen for him: his friends did manage his risk for him when he wanted to 'be the normal guy he once was'. He knew his success gave incredible freedoms, but it also reduced the 'everyman' spur-of-the-moment events many of us take for granted. If he ever forgot his place – and he tried often – his friends were there to remind him.

I took this experience away with me and didn't think on it too much. I was not sure there was a lot to learn from it, but I was wrong. The greater the responsibility, the more likely is the aversion to risk. Personally, we live this as we grow to be parents and professionally it extends to co-workers, through to employees. In the case of the billionaire, it extends to thousands of employees, shareholders and their families. Now, I draw upon this and when speaking to yacht owners I am more sensitive to their increased responsibilities, and allow them to set the level. If they want to be the 'everyman' and take themselves to the edge of risk, I assume, very timidly, the role of my previous employer's friends: just adding a little brake to the exuberance they had 'way back when'.

I also learned that the outward-facing decision may not represent the inward. My billionaire was kind to share that he was hungry, happy to take the counsel of his friends and was not upset. By his choosing to explain these points, I was given the insight. This is rare and it is more likely that in any personal and professional interaction the cause for a particular decision will not be given so freely and to ask may be indiscreet. I now in the first instance just respect the decision, for it is theirs; maybe this becomes a prompt for them to share, or maybe it does not.

Judging risk

You may not understand why a decision is made. This is OK, it is not about you.

Personal risk comes in many forms, and we all see it differently. Physical risk is the most visible but emotional and intellectual risk are harder to see: try to keep a broad view when judging or even setting the risk profile of others.

Driving Miss Daisy

I love emergencies. I love seeing how I and those around me respond in the real-time pressure that an emergency creates. I love the elevated intensity that an emergency brings. It was what first drew me to ocean racing; there is no time to have a slice of orange and talk through what happens in the next quarter of the game. When the weather is heavy, decisions need to be made fast, and they have real consequences. Often, the approach to a decision is not governed by the weight of the decision; rather, it is the time available to make it that is the driving factor.

Sailing as a superyacht captain is not ocean racing, but I have found myself fully tested by the emergencies that have come my way. Each time I was aware that my decisions were needed in the moment, there was little counsel available, and my judgements would be irreversible. Maybe it is a flaw in my character that sees this challenge with consequence as appealing.

My emergencies have happened fast and slow. It has always been the choice of the emergency and not me as to what the pace will be. I think that early in my career, if I had been given the choice, I would have leaned to the slow emergency as my preference, more *Driving Miss Daisy* and less *Fast & Furious*. Over time, I have had cause to question this. If I must have a favourite, I have warmed to the fast-flowing emergency.

Early in my captaincy career, I experienced emergencies and near emergencies without loss of life. This was luck, as I knew I had not handled them well enough, there were gaps, and if I did not improve, something terrible would happen. The answer seemed simple: learn more; work harder. I had to build a system to guarantee I had every ounce of knowledge available to me at all times. This was a good base, but I realised that knowledge alone would not be enough, and to successfully tackle a major emergency I needed to have such confidence that I was able to operate intuitively. I set about achieving this through visualisation and so many drills that I was capable of taking actions based as much on muscle memory as deliberate thought. During an emergency I needed the mental room to receive all the inputs coming my way: like a sportsperson or a driver in a race, the level at which I sought to function was informed instinct.

I think of cricketers, batsmen, being interviewed and their description of looking to the pace bowler's fingers as they are about to unleash a small and hard ball at them at close to 100 miles per hour from 22 yards away. Faced with this, I would cower, soil myself or both. World-class batsmen luckily do neither and move instinctively from research and repetition. I never invested time in cricket as a youth, but now as a captain I needed to apply the same process as the batsmen to effectively slow down time when the fast emergency flies at me like the ball from the bowler's fingers. Unlike the batsmen in my sporting metaphor, the emergency does not give the good grace of a run-up to watch it develop. It is hidden from view, embedded in each day unseen until the last instant, when it chooses to make itself known...

The yacht was ready to set to sea from St Nazaire in France after completing a six-month refit. St Nazaire is awash with shipping industry and through history its fortunes have ebbed and flowed with the economy of shipbuilding. The Chantiers de l'Atlantique in its various forms have a long and incredibly proud history. Their constructions include *Queen Mary II* and *Harmony of the Seas*, with the latter measuring a jaw-dropping 362 metres in length. In addition to these modern achievements, there is the ever present reminder of darker times, with the network of submarine pens built for use by the German U-boat forces in the Second World War.

This history was not known to me on the morning of the yacht's arrival. Alongside the other captain, I had spoken out against the choice of St Nazaire as the location for the refit as (in yachting terms) it was remote, with little yachting infrastructure, and we were to be supported by only a small team from Marseille. The strategy was to work from demountable containers placed on the dock adjacent to the yacht, with only the trades needed for each stage of the works on site. To both captains, this was a significant departure from our previous experiences of a successful project and we pushed back with our concerns. Sometimes it is wonderful to be proved wrong, and through a combination of good planning and good project management, the refit was a complete success. There is something to be said for having a lean team of talented professionals and making the administration follow the work and not the reverse.

A key responsibility of the captain and crew was the series of critical tests needed prior to departure. The bridge had been completely upgraded and I, along with the bridge team, undertook responsibility to develop and complete a rigorous set-to-work regime. This would, in a new construction, be the builder's responsibility, but given a good depth of experience a schedule of testing was developed by the crew and shared with the yacht's Flag Registry for their endorsement.

All equipment had to be powered up, used in every configuration, then shut down in different sequences and the process then duplicated with back-up systems. This was repeated and repeated again with as much load from the propellers as was safe with the yacht afloat in the now flooded dry dock. After several weeks of such testing, escalating to full failure drills, the team were prepared. I felt confident in the quality of the equipment, the installation team, and my own and the crew's ability to take any action required in the event of an emergency. With this, I reported to the yacht's management and owners that the yacht could proceed to sea.

The extensive dock and basin areas in St Nazaire are located on the bank of the Loire River. The Loire is tidal, with ranges of up to 5 metres. To achieve the correct tidal conditions, the yacht needed to depart the Chantiers de l'Atlantique dock, passage through the inner Bassin de

Penhoët and then through another dock, the Louis Joubert, before finally reaching the Loire River. The St Nazaire port authority visited the yacht in the week prior to departure and through their own risk management process advised that they required the yacht to have two harbour tugs on standby until the yacht had cleared the outer lock. This was a standard precaution and I willingly adhered to the port's direction. Given the value and delicacy of the paintwork, it was requested the tugs remain only on standby, rather than connecting. Again, there was broad agreement. The departure date arrived, and the time given by the port authority was driven by the need to meet slack high water as the yacht reached the outer dock. Slack high water refers to when the tide is cresting and is neither running into the port (flooding) nor running out (ebbing). We needed this stability in the water column to ensure we departed the lock without being pushed to one side or the other, risking damage. Tidal flows are less visible than wind, but have an approximate tenfold impact on the ship.

It was a cold, early spring morning and for once I was appreciative of the yacht's enclosed bridge wings. I could see the deck crew on the foredeck stamping their feet and blowing into cupped hands to keep warm. All the team had to stand by for the departure from the first dry dock, our temporary home for the past six months, through the basin and then again through the outer lock, which was our last barrier to the Loire River. This took just over two hours and once the yacht was in the Loire River channel the tugs were released, and the deck crew were able to come into the yacht and warm up. Two crew stood by anchors in case there was an emergency and the anchors needed to be let go. This is standard practice, and all were relieved as the most challenging part of the day had been completed without fuss.

I had spent many hours over the past weeks visualising this entire manoeuvre. Experience adds value; I knew what it was to undertake something that was poorly planned, and I didn't wish to test my luck again. I walked the docks and looked at the basin from all perspectives during afternoon runs that I strategically planned to provide me with views of the port facility. My favourite route involved ascending the stairs of the former submarine pens, where I could see the entire port. I also stood on the elevated aft decks of the yacht and moved my hands through the motions of the control levers, visualising each critical point of the manoeuvres. I knew I must have looked daft, but I didn't care. After this I would return to the bridge and repeat with the actual controls; they had electrical power but no control over propulsion and I would transfer between control stations, simulate failures and move the levers to the positions I thought I would need. It felt good on completion of the port departure that all this practice meant the execution was virtually an anti-climax. I didn't need to revert to redundant systems and the critical points I had lain awake contemplating passed without incident.

The harbour pilot had monitored the tides closely all morning. He had asked me to increase speed through the basin and then held the yacht in the second lock for a little longer to ensure on departing the lock gates that the water was truly 'slack'. We slipped out of the Louis Joubert dock with no effect from the tide. We had been well served by a professional pilot and I thanked him as he departed and the river pilot joined. It is not unusual to change pilots for different phases, but it breaks the flow of the team and we held position just south of the lock to conduct a new briefing with the river pilot. We had done our own research and could have departed independently. Regardless, the bridge team gave their full attention as the pilot briefed on the local environment and his preference for speeds in the river channel.

The departure, once clear of the port, is simple: one turn to the south-west and then follow a well-marked channel that is kept dredged for commercial shipping to 13 metres (our draught was a mere 6 metres). The river outside of the channel in these first 8 miles was muddy, with some patches drying. At the end of the river the yacht would reach open water, a point where, even outside the channel, there was enough water for safe navigation.

The pilot glanced at his watch and told me that the tide would start ebbing very soon so I would need to be mindful of this. I always appreciate this local knowledge, and I gratefully acknowledged him. With awareness that the tidal flow would be increasing, I confirmed that the yacht could enter the channel. In addition to the local environmental conditions, the pilot is also aware of, and in communications with, the other ships in the area. In this case, the pilot advised there was a bulk ship entering from the sea and we would meet them in the channel. The waterway was 300 metres wide and designed for ships to pass within it; there was no concern with this inbound ship. The only other comment the pilot made was to note that the ship was on the incoming tide and was travelling at 14 knots. The pilot's assessment was that the ship had 3 knots of flood tide under it. (The movement of the tide may seem contradictory, that we have a high water that is soon to start flowing out and at the same time another ship entering the port on a flood tide flowing in. Tides are complicated and it is not uncommon that there will be several different tidal events on the same river at the same time.)

The day had warmed to a very pleasant Atlantic spring morning and the mood was buoyant. The yacht was greatly improved from the works period and we were all looking forward to returning to the cruising schedule. Due to the size of the yacht, all bridge officers were commercially trained. This provides no guarantee of professionalism over yacht-trained bridge officers, but the bridge operates in accordance with practice familiar to the pilot. This is not lip service to the pilot, but it was an important safety benefit that the behaviours and orders on the yacht's bridge reflected his normal trading ship environment. The helmsman is an essential member of this team, and for this important departure we had chosen a long-serving crew member. He had trained during the harbour trials and I knew he was instinctively familiar with all controls and emergency procedures.

As the yacht completed the turn into the Loire River channel, I increased the engine settings to achieve 8 knots. I was beginning to feel the tidal flow on the yacht and in these conditions having waterflow over the rudders is key to maintaining control. There is a temptation in early ship handling that 'slow is safe', often spoken as 'go slow like a pro'. This is not possible in strong tides or winds; ships and motor yachts can only steer when water flows over their rudders and the way to achieve this is by putting power to the propellers in a measured manner.

As the speed increased, the pilot and the chief officer were both communicating to me in a relaxed manner, both sharing their observations of the yacht's position and the effects of the tide. We were on our outbound heading on the starboard side of the channel. The inbound ship was visible and identified on the radar and visually as the MV *Eternal Salute*. The ship was a dry bulk carrier, length 228 metres, beam 38 metres and a gross tonnage of 47,000 tonnes. Mirroring our placement, the *Eternal Salute* was correctly placed on the starboard side of the channel from their inbound perspective. This is the equivalent to both ships being in their lanes on the motorway, a simple yet essential part of safety in confined waters.

The pilot suggested the yacht increase speed to improve handling: we had moved out into the river and due to a local counter current (an eddy) our speed had slowed to 6 knots. I agreed with the pilot and ordered 12 knots. I did not expect we would achieve 12: 9–10 knots was the target. There was a professional ease on the bridge after the hours of intensity during departure. The steward visited and I was appreciative of the cup of tea he offered. The yacht passed 8 knots; this was announced by the helmsman, and I acknowledged his report. Over a sip of tea, I saw the *Eternal Salute* continuing in our direction, less than a mile away now and well placed on the south-eastern side of the channel. We remained well positioned, passing a marker buoy on the north-western side at a range of 30 metres.

'Ship not responding to the helm.'

The alert from the helmsman was made just as the yacht started to turn at an increasing rate to port, across the channel. In the time it took for his words to be spoken, the yacht's heading was turning at 20 degrees per minute and this rate was increasing speed all the time. As a result of our extensive drills, I was able to direct the helmsman to change through each descending layer of back-up steering. The chief officer and the pilot stood near me at the centreline, but none of my actions had any effect on the rudders: they were pinned at 10 degrees to port and the yacht was now mid-channel and the rate of turn was passing 40 degrees per minute. This rate of turn was uncomfortably fast for a large vessel; the horizon was racing.

The pilot was highly animated, and in a voice that had changed to a higher pitch was loudly instructing me to turn to starboard and return to the northern side of the channel. As intimately as the pilot knew the Loire River, he did not know the yacht, and I knew that with this rate of turn there was no chance of stopping and reversing with a turn to starboard. The name *Eternal Salute* was now clearly visible on the bow of the inbound bulk carrier; it was 40 degrees off the yacht's bow and, relative to our position, was moving swiftly. The subsequent review using the vessel's data recorder showed the ship to be three ship lengths away and on a collision course at this moment. I did not know this precise detail at the time, but I could see the rust streaks adjacent to the ship's anchor and knew instinctively we were closing on a steady bearing towards collision.

I was assessing all options in real time. Reducing speed might be part of the solution and the pilot was calling to me repeatedly, 'Captain, Captain, stop the ship.' If I did that, I knew the tidal stream would take the yacht to mid-channel and would not solve our risk of collision with the *Eternal Salute*; I ignored the pilot's repeated demands. There were two choices at this point as I saw them, and neither were good. We could collide with the inbound ship or run aground on the mudflats.

I made the decision; aground on mud is terrible, but better than another ship. I began the actions to execute this plan. Actions were needed more than discussion; the time to seek shared agreement had passed. I barked to the pilot to contact his colleague on *Eternal Salute* and have him alter his ship to port and move to the north of the channel. The pilot resisted fleetingly as it was in contradiction to accepted international practice. I had a plan and was committing to it and needed the pilot to play his role. I would like to think I was drawing upon my deep knowledge of the collision avoidance rules that under special circumstances allow for a departure from their instructions. The reality was that I was acting automatically, using my knowledge of what the yacht could achieve when asked.

The pilot saw *Eternal Salute* on the yacht's starboard beam and closing: there was no chance of our returning to starboard. He called the other ship, his high-pitched voice breaking:

'*Salute, Salute,* this is... Turn to port, turn to port directement!'

I saw *Eternal Salute* turning to port and the two short blasts from their baritone whistle confirmed their intentions. They had read the situation and were taking action from their own judgement. Concurrent with the pilot's call and *Eternal Salute* turning away, I had moved the helmsman from the conning station and was manhandling the controls. I knew what was needed and did not wish to delay by using the normal command and response conning. This circumvented one of the key monitoring points in a functioning bridge team, but it was not the classroom and I needed to take action.

Moving to the controls allowed me to communicate my decisions to the bridge team in a narrative and not just by conning orders. I finally shared my awareness of the two options I had seen and that I had chosen the latter. The first was collision with the inbound ship and the second was grounding on the mud banks. There was a collective intake of breath as the reality of what we were facing sank in. We were likely to ground, and the captain had consciously chosen this.

The chief officer, who had so far been more observer than actor, now found his role. He spoke to the anchor party on his internal radio and made sure they were ready. He instructed the officer of the watch to check all watertight doors (the essential barriers to stop full-length flooding) were closed: they were. I asked him to tell the engineers what we were planning; they were blind to our situation and would soon be confronted by multiple concerns. The engineers in the next two minutes would likely face hull damage, stability changes and blackouts from mud blocking generator cooling intakes. I was using bow thrusters and engines to speed the turn; we were passing 60 degrees a minute and the yacht was leaning over angrily. The chief officer and I caught each other's eye and simultaneously said, 'Stabilisers'. We were running through checklists in our minds, faster than the officer of the watch could follow with the printed version. The stabilisers were extended and presented a huge risk of piercing the hull if we were to ground. The 'retract' button was adjacent the bow thruster and I pushed it among my other actions, trying to short-turn the yacht in the channel.

Looking at the camera screen above my head, I could see *Eternal Salute* passing very close, but safely, through our stern and that there would be no collision. Looking ahead, I could see clearly the white lettering '15' atop the green channel marker. With some surprise, I realised we had almost completed the 180-degree turn and remained inside the channel. As I put the engines astern and the bow thrusters to starboard,

I steadied the yacht with the channel marker 5 degrees on the starboard bow and we stood safely in the channel.

In three and a half minutes, we had worked together to reverse the course of the yacht in the channel and stop. The chief officer asked if I wanted to drop anchors: it was a good suggestion, but I preferred to get to open seas. Influencing my decision, the steering control had unaccountably returned, and my feeling was that whatever the fault, the best place to fully determine its cause and repair would be in open water.

The chief electrician had been on the bridge within the first 30 seconds of the emergency and was on the internal phone to the second electrician in the steering gear room and checking all that they could. He was a great electrician and combined with the wider engineering team I felt we had the best team to resolve the emergency on board.

I had not spoken with the pilot since our terse exchange and my direction to call the inbound ship that went against his preferred path. I sought to repair our master/pilot relationship and apologised. To his credit the pilot said he was wrong, and we had followed the only option available. With the mood now returned to calm, I asked the pilot again to assist, and could he call the tugs to escort the yacht to safe water.

The tugs returned and with trepidation we proceeded to sea by reversing course and resuming our original track. Everything was working but there was an enormous shadow: there was no defined cause of why the failure had occurred and why all back-up modes were not successful. With the combined attention of the manufacturers and all engineering team members, it took four days to finally determine it was a speed-sensitive relay that was malfunctioning and locking the steering whenever the yacht reached 9 knots. A relay that was not shown on drawings and was not even known to be in place.

I am still near to shaking at the remembrance of just how close it came. The day after the departure, one of the Nepalese deck crew saw me and said, 'Captain, you are so good at driving this ship. How you knew the other ship would pass 40 metres behind us was amazing.' He had no idea of what had been going on and presumed the *Eternal Salute* passing that close was by design. I asked him how he knew it was so close. He said he was on the aft mooring station packing things away and looked up to wave to a deck rating on the other ship. As I thanked him for his compliment, my knees trembled. It was only a few seconds' difference between his waving to the other ship and the bow of the *Eternal Salute* tearing through the starboard quarter and him being crushed.

There are many incidents that I have grown from, but that time in the Loire River may be the single greatest maritime learning moment of my career. It was certainly the greatest validation of my belief in the requirement for unconscious competence in all aspects of emergency actions. Those weeks prior to departure from St Nazaire where I had stolen time each day to go to the bridge alone saved the ship that day. The controls were new, and the only way I knew how to handle them during this fast-flowing emergency was the time spent standing at each of the three conning positions and visualising the departure and what I would expect to do with the control levers. I had developed a muscle memory for their placement and the weight of resistance each control lever had. The bow thrusters were very light, and it was easy to place more power than expected, whereas the main engine control levers were heavier and needed a forceful action. I also went through 'touch drills' on every back-up system following my internal flow chart of 'if this... then what?' I would approach the conning position from different angles, close my eyes and reach for a control lever to test I knew its location instinctively.

This preparation was less about an expectation of a failure – I had the utmost confidence in the system, its configuration and its installation – and more that I was self-conscious of my own abilities and needed to make myself bulletproof in the execution of this core competence. It is with no hyperbole that this approach saved lives: we had 99 crew and passengers that day. If I had had to fumble for controls and think about back-up systems, the extra seconds would have been lost and a 90-degree 'T-bone' collision would have been almost guaranteed.

I have had many control system failures since St Nazaire, but whether it was drawn upon or not, I have repeated that preparation over and over. I realised there was no time to be learning when the emergency was happening. Often cited as a soldier's creed, I found this quote motivating and transferrable:

'In the thick of battle, you will not rise to the level of your expectations, but fall to the level of your training.'

In his book *Bounce*, the former Olympian Matthew Syed breaks the narrative of elite performance being the domain of the talented or genetically gifted in firm agreement with the unnamed soldier whose creed is cited above. Syed breaks down success from Picasso to Mozart to The Beatles and, of course, multiple sports champions. He proposes that champions are not born – they are made through practice. Aside from enjoying reading the book, I found it truly empowering; it meant that, with practice, I too could be elite at something. This is not some folly; I will not be running the 100 metres in the Olympics, but within my own physical limitations I could reach a high standard by clever and consistent practice. I needed this elite performance to overcome the fast-flowing emergency.

Sadly, rapid responses based on repetitive training and muscle memory do not transfer directly to a slow emergency. Slow emergencies are insidious and are affected by our biology, which focuses on the immediate and allows the longer-term, though more consequential, to not receive the same attention. This proximity effect, where we respond to what is visible and clearly defined as a risk, yet ignore the horizon, is most clearly and tragically present on a global scale with the apathy towards climate change. Even the most aware struggle to associate a cause and effect, linking their plastic-wrapped sandwich to a global crisis. In contrast, when a child runs towards a street, the action and the effect are linked in a matter of seconds. This also extends to the proximity of the decision maker to the effects of their decision. The aged, climate change-denying politician is not as invested in the emergency as the parent running to save their child.

My deep belief in repetitive practice has actually hindered my success in handling slow emergencies. These require awareness, learning, reflection, patience and strategy. I can deliver on a couple of these in isolation but falter in bringing them all to the fore: my yearning to solve the problem and swiftly return all to order works against my success.

Like many slow emergencies, defining the beginning is difficult: there is often no real event that can be reviewed, and here there was no crash as something broke, just a slow creep.

Alcohol at sea is a perennial and difficult subject. The written obligations for alcohol consumption are as black and white in their prescriptive manner as the ink that beds them to the pages of the Safety Management System. This system is written a long way from the yacht by authors who are as equal in their well-meaning intent as they are in their lack of awareness of life at sea. Regardless of their genesis, the laws are not mine to interpret; there is very little in the maritime sphere that is optional – captains are to uphold and implement. I have through my career held a firm line that I do not have the right to ignore these regulations: the crew must live with alcohol restrictions. For my own part, I have moved to where I do not consume alcohol at sea; it is much easier to make a personal rule than to assess each exception. I could not allow myself to be the cliché headline when the inevitable accident occurs.

I know this is unpopular and I know it is not upheld by many of my peers. To be honest, I wish I did not feel the need to uphold the regulations and that responsibility could be devolved to each person to make the correct decision at the correct time. This is not the reality, and I always knew I could not delegate the unpalatable regulations for my own ease. I know the risk/consequence ratio is very high and have heard myself say too many times, 'I will not be making the phone call to a loved one of a crew member to tell them their child, partner, parent will not be returning home due to an alcohol-related accident. An accident that I contributed to by not upholding an unpopular policy.'

I carried this view as I met with a young yacht-owning couple at their Bel Air residence to learn their expectations prior to my joining their yacht for the first time as their captain. Irrespective of my own maritime obligations, their direction was clear. The yacht is a workplace, and alcohol has no role in a functioning workplace. I suggested that some easing of this hard-line position, in accordance with maritime law, would assist. I used the analogy of a spring under pressure, and it being better to ease it gently than to let it snap. The unattractive reality is that when crew are 'dry' at sea, their first days ashore live to the trope this image presents. It also presents the captain with an incredible risk as crew disregard their own safety in the pursuit of 'making up for lost time'.

Listening openly, the yacht owners acquiesced, and we agreed to a set of 'rules' to safely serve alcohol on board that were achievable and within the legal framework. Once on board, I held an all-crew meeting to introduce myself and to share that I was in this with them; we had engaged yacht owners with a strong vision and a wish to travel the globe and we were in a very fortunate position. Embedded in this warm and positive initial briefing were some ground rules; some were repeating what was in place and some were new. I was aware that all my positive messaging would be loosely listened to and the crew would be focused on any curtailment of their lifestyle on board. I laid out the plan I had recently agreed with the owners: alcohol was only to be served under captain's supervision. It was to be a defined event and no more than three drinks per person. I gained no immediate feedback after delivering the message.

Weeks and then months passed under the regime. I allowed it to go on auto, I never sought to be the policeman, and when asked to approve a social event on board I defaulted to yes. There was a record kept of drinks consumed and the chief stewardess would send me a copy the following morning. I always looked at it and always responded to her messages, but I never physically checked.

I was busy, the system never caused me any problems, so I did not challenge it. Most evenings I would retire to my cabin to read, literally exhausted after 15 hours or more of interacting with crew and/or guests. I would retreat and enjoy the solace of my solitude. I had my inner circle within the crew that I had come to rely on, and through this felt I had the insight I needed into how the yacht was functioning. My theory was flawed: it was based on a group that was too homogeneous. My insight was from those I worked most closely with and some others who joined me for group fitness out of hours. By spending time with only the crew I enjoyed sharing time with, I had omitted those who needed my leadership most.

We did not know but the new owners and I had inherited a yacht that under previous ownership and previous captaincy had partied hard and often. I knew from whispered confessions that, even in the senior group, some preferred the 'old days'. I did not seek to chase this actively as to do so would have meant confronting an issue that I felt I did not have time for. I suspected that if I looked, I would likely discover a group who were in breach both of legal obligations and the wishes of the new owner.

This was an emergency unfolding with such a slow creep that nobody even noticed. Each unsupervised event pushed things a little further until my lack of clear guidance and monitoring allowed such loose interpretations of the rules that newly joined crew did not know where their boundaries were. They did not have the historical reference, and nor did I refresh this narrative to the crew: the why was missing and with this the crew were following (or not) rules with no sense of them being anchored in legal and moral obligations. This is not even to acknowledge and restate the yacht owner's wishes. Within yachting, it is the latter that must be considered as being equal to the regulatory obligations.

What was worse, with some honest reflection I knew it was developing and did not want to deal with it. As the first to wake most mornings, I noticed the crew mess bin fuller than it should have been, beer and wine bottles poking their necks out. I noticed crew who were bleary-eyed, and I chose not to address it. I justified this by saying to the senior crew that I trusted their judgement. 'Senior' is a relative term and although most of the crew in senior roles had professional competence, I knew some of their emotional maturity was not up to the responsibility I had asked of them. Again, nothing was really going wrong so I could indulge myself in this little self-deception to make for a better night's sleep. Like a swell in deep sea, the energy that will become a wave crashing ashore is there, but the impact is not even visible. Indeed, a deep ocean swell is one of the most peaceful things to watch and gives no hint of the mayhem it may bring as it comes to the shore. My wave crashed one quiet evening in a remote area.

The yacht had been at anchor for an extended period and one of the 'supervised' events devolved into a large party that then retreated to crew cabins to maintain the subterfuge of secrecy. There was a late-night drunken fight and drug use. The response of those involved was a textbook play for the survival of the greater group. My firmness against excessive alcohol and zero tolerance for drug use was known and a wall against the truth was built by those who I relied on to represent the facts with integrity. The drug use was said to be isolated and blamed on two of the youngest in the crew, who were then dismissed in the morning. What this did not address was the tension that remained within the crew between the 'rule followers' and the 'partygoers' and this did not dissipate. The cohesion within the team was terminally broken and those that did not seek to leave soon after only remained due to the lack of an equivalent opportunity.

In the aftermath of the 'event', as it became referred to in termination and formal warning letters, the fault continued to be laid against the junior crew who were now long departed. Were they at fault at all? Was it instead the fault of my lax monitoring, and over-reliance on crew who I knew didn't hold the emotional maturity and fortitude to uphold a policy that was in conflict with an earlier, deeply ingrained and preferred party culture?

I carried out the actions I was obliged to: career-ending terminations, written warnings and, in some cases, professional emotional counselling. This followed all the terms of employment contracts and was supported by all managers ashore. Technically I played it 'by the book' and there was no failing in my actions, but my lack of strategy to deal with the slow emergency had an impact. What those sitting in offices far away did not see was the up-close shock on young lives that the 'event' caused. I saw this, and my former nights of sound slumber became a memory. I struggled to read as I thought of the effect on those who had been summarily dismissed and whose names were blighted. These were not crew on a payroll or names on an employment contract, these were my shipmates, and their loss was real to me, as was my inaction in the time preceding the 'event'. I also reflected that those who I had relied on for truth had constructively conspired to build a lie, to protect themselves at the expense of others.

Slow emergencies need strategies, and I was caught out by dealing with each event as an independent problem and, worse, recognising it and taking no action. This was wrong. I should have linked behaviours and events, developed a plan and implemented it to overcome what was a systemic problem. What should I have done differently? I think a lot about this, and I should have assessed where the crew culture was before I joined, where it was at that moment, and where it was heading. I did not invest this time and spent the days largely on autopilot, moving across each issue as it presented. If you asked me at the end of the day what strategy I had engaged, I would draw a blank. I had sold myself on the myth that the crew would all follow my message just because I had said it. I denied myself the truth that people behave following their own, often irrational, set of justifications and the leader needs to be present to reinforce the message.

To approach this situation again, I would map a time each day to engage and determine where the cultural touchpoints were for the crew, and what actually mattered for them. I was more than 20 years older than the majority and my personal views were out of touch. Like compound interest, this daily learning would have delivered a huge knowledge reward but only well after investing the time. I should have worked harder to develop a more diverse truth-circle on board and listened to their comments more closely. I did not need to attend every function, but I needed to attend more than I did, and not view this as being the policeman but rather as a chance to relax and enjoy the company of the team in a more intimate setting. Had I made these small investments and journaled the small pieces of learning, I would have never left the team so exposed to the slow emergency of their own doing.

To be better prepared for slow emergencies, I have learned the importance of taking action very early. When you smell the smoke, you take action before the flames are upon you. One former captain confusingly advised, 'When you are in doubt it is too late. You must take action when you are in doubt that you are in doubt.' The slow emergency begins on the day when nothing untoward happens, and this is the day I should have invested my time 'listening to learn'.

Emergencies, fast and slow

Fast:
Careful attention to practice will make you an expert in a field that you are suited to become an expert in.
Slow:
Leadership and cultural emergencies need a nuanced strategy and a much longer investment. It begins on the day that nothing happens, and it never stops.

Listen to others – really listen – and note the slightest shifts in behaviour.

Ego is the enemy

As with the weather, ship handling is a popular conversation among yacht captains/yacht professionals. The ports are small and seemingly shrinking as yacht size increases. Overlaid is that while commercial shipping tolerates a gentle 'slide' along a dock, given that the paint on yachts reaches into tens of millions of dollars, this luxury is not available to a superyacht captain.

On this particular day, the yacht was over 120 metres in length and drew 6 metres of water, so it was very tight entering the ancient Port Vauban in Antibes, where clearance was measured in half metres. To support this, tools had been put in place in the port, and a measuring instrument called a fan beam had been installed. Fan beams are used extensively in the oil and gas industry to provide precise positioning information to allow service ships to approach the oil platforms. In this case, the unit on the dock reflected a laser off the yacht and measured the distance to a centimetre. This provided a precise position to allow its dynamic positioning system to allocate thrust accurately. The operator must still define the settings and where the yacht should go, but if the parameters are entered correctly, the precise reference in companion with the dynamic positioning algorithm will move the ship to the desired position.

I had been trained and had experience using the dynamic positioning system. There are captains who see this technology as a threat, or do not understand its capabilities and limitations. I am neither: I see it as an exceptional tool to facilitate precise ship handling in confined conditions. Having said this, ship handling is fun, and in the weeks leading up to this port entry I had had a flurry of opportunity for manually driving the yacht and I thought it would be 'fun' to do this port entry in full manual.

Co-working, and specifically co-captaincy, is an intimate relationship to the point of being symbiotic, your own performance being reliant on that of your colleague. You take over their workplace and inherit their successes and their failures as your own. There are not too many career situations where two senior managers share the same role at the same time, and it is almost closer to parenting than a normal workplace. There have been times when I look to the pressures placed on senior corporate or political leaders and wonder whether having two to fulfil the expectations could be a wise solution. My former co-captains remain my closest friends in the yachting community; we share a moment in time, and we draw upon this to underwrite our friendships. Among this group is Glenn, who I rang with my thoughts on entering Port Vauban.

Glenn had interviewed me for the captain's role and was the senior in our relationship. We shared a fantastic camaraderie as peers, though I never shook that I was beholden to him for the wonderful opportunity to serve as the captain. For his part, he never played that card and treated me entirely as his equal.

The yacht had anchored to make final preparations for port entry, and I called for support. This was the first time I had entered the harbour and speaking with my co-captain was both to show respect for his experience and to gain some insight into this difficult port entry. Glenn had entered yachting from the world of deep-sea cable laying and was a very competent dynamic positioning operator: he leaned on this system heavily, but also knew its limitations.

I shared with him my plan to bring the yacht into port under full manual control. I led into it with a light-hearted tone and the word 'fun' was included. There was a pause before his response. He was mature in conversation and did not initially leap to criticise, but instead repeated back to me some of the key points I had just shared and explored my reasoning for this choice. He drew gently but firmly to his point and I recall specifically his message: 'Brendan, if you bring your ego to the bridge you are taking a big step closer to having an accident.' I absorbed this and drew breath without responding, which was just as well as he wasn't finished.

'When you own your own €400 million yacht you can indulge your wishes. Until that time you need to constantly assess how to minimise risk. Taking the yacht into Port Vauban in full manual is not minimising risk.'

The words on the page make this look like a firm rebuke, but it wasn't. It was peer mentoring and peer truth.

I absorbed my colleague's comments and I used all automation available to me to bring the yacht into this very constrained port safely. Glenn's message transcended the bridge and I have worked to apply his advice in life. It is not a yacht captain's unique insight not to approach life with your ego leading, but it was the context and the risk that brought it home.

Look out for your ego

It is rare you will recognise your ego leading you towards adversity and/or failure or hindering you from your outcome. You are deep inside your own reality and it takes real effort to step outside to see if your decision-making is rational, based on an objective view, or rational but based on placing you in the centre.

Even the most noble exploits often have ego at their centre – and this is OK, so long as you sense it and check in that it is not hindering the outcome before proceeding.

Try and build a trusted path for someone to point it out to you: as much as it will be shielded for you, it will be on display for others.

Is that Santa?

There is no way to achieve excellence without commitment. This is not too great a leap to embrace and the term 'leap' is not chosen by accident. I give all I have, and when I run, ride or ski it is as fast as I can. It may not even be very fast, but it is the fastest I can go on that day. This is a terrible system and I seem to perpetually pendulum from training to injury, and back. In the workplace I suffer the same affliction and have learned that giving 100 per cent commitment has at times been a burden and even a barrier to my success.

One afternoon in the Maldives....

The Maldives archipelago is fundamentally organised to move guests from the airport to their resorts and to reverse this on completion of their holiday. Between the two transfers, the resorts aim to provide as many opportunities as possible to have their guests spend more than they had intended at their time of booking. I may be oversimplifying luxury travel, but this is my observation.

Under this premise, the choices to spend only increase each time I visit. Fine dining, fine dining under water, fine dining in an observatory, diving, diving with sharks, pampering, pampering under water, flying, boating...

with the most noble of all the indulgent pursuits being an engagement with the environment.

The resorts are working hard to improve their social and environmental credibility and are doing so with sea life rescue and breeding. With no judgement on the corporate motivations of these endeavours, they do provide much-needed funding for marine sciences in the abundant – or, in many areas, formerly abundant – waters. Speaking to marine biologists and interns at the turtle recovery sanctuaries, there is a sense that regardless of the motivations, the outcome is a good thing. Among all this, the Maldives Whale Shark Research Programme stands out, in my opinion, in its scope and truth in purpose. It has been operating since 2006 and is committed to the goals of supporting the conservation of whale sharks in Maldives waters and furthering global understanding of these incredible animals.

To reflect the guests' interest in the environment and to provide an incredible experience, we approached the research team. The lead marine biologists would come to the yacht and present on whale sharks and their own studies. I found these presentations gripping; we do not know very much about these giants and those studying whale sharks are the first to admit our knowledge is based on minimal data. After the presentations, the next phase was the wonder of seeing them. The plan was we would take two biologists in our small boats with the guests, and a third would go in the helicopter as spotter. The rules on viewing whale sharks are clear and followed by all credible operators; the biologists would ensure the boats and swimmers stayed in defined safe areas so as not to impact on these wonderful creatures.

I received the call the next morning from our contact at the charity. She shared in an excited voice that there had been a pod of whale sharks sighted and would we be ready to get moving in the tenders in the next hour? This was grand news, and I faced my next challenge: even with the promise of whale sharks, could I create the energy within the guest group to mobilise in the next hour? Whatever I said, it worked, and we had movement.

The yacht was anchored in a sheltered inner atoll bay on the western side of Dhidhdhoo. It is a beautiful location but not without its challenges: the charts are inconsistently in error, that is, the amount and direction of the error varies. Marvellous. This results in the unsettling situation for a captain where the ship's position is never quite certain. Aside from natural beauty and navigational excitement, the choice of location was determined by the known swimming path of the whale sharks, just to the south of Maamigili, the southernmost island of South Ari Atoll.

The team from the research programme arrived in their boat and transferred to our tenders. One of the biologists remained with me on the yacht and we would be the spotters from the helicopter. As with the restrictions to the boats, there were flight restrictions in place to safeguard the whale sharks. I am not 100 per cent sure what about a helicopter does or does not upset a whale shark and who found it out, but for the sake of good tourist citizenship we willingly abided by all obligations. The helicopter launched from the deck and established communications with the tenders. The air and water were both so clear we were already seeing smaller reef fish and sharks as we flew past. Helicopters are rare in the Maldives and the other tour operators knew to follow to share the advantage.

The pilot, François, was former French military and in parallel to conscientiousness was always willing to engage in some theatre to entertain the guests if it did not compromise safety. We had spoken before take-off and I had shared my idea: it was approaching Christmas and I thought the experience for the guests would be increased by their spotter – me – wearing a Santa suit. There were children in the guest group, I was missing my own daughters, and I thought it might be fun. I did have some other ideas, but I thought I would wait until we were airborne before bringing it up.

Flying high above the fringing atoll is just magnificent. Being much faster than the tenders, the helicopter had extra time, and on the guidance of the biologist we looped west of Fenfushi island to look at the fringe reef. It was so clear we could even see the grey reef sharks that normally blend so well across the sands of the fringing atoll – beautiful. As it was morning, François wanted to loop back to the east to put the sun over our shoulder and to be in our whale shark safe place – that is, behind the tenders, looking forward of them. It was about a seven-minute traverse, and I used the time to propose my idea. Simple concept: once we had finished spotting the whale sharks, I could pay homage to some of my former naval experience and leap from the helicopter in my Santa suit. I thought it would be a real treat for the kids to wave at Santa as I leapt into the water, and I had a few sweets in a waterproof satchel I had brought with me to round out the novelty. True to my judgement, François thought this was a great plan and had done many diver drops in his military career. I was maintaining an external ease, but I was excited. I like jumping into the water from any height and from a helicopter just adds another layer of fun.

We spent 40 minutes directing the guests. The effectiveness was reinforced by our biologist, also in the helicopter, who, giddy with it all, said we had seen more whale sharks in one outing than in a normal month. With her 300-millimetre lens, she was busy photographing each animal and in most cases being able to name the whale through its markings. It was a total success; we could hear the hoots of the guests over the radio as they leapt to and from the water as each new whale was spotted. The boat in use was a 12-metre catamaran with a bow ramp that was lowered just above the water to give ease of access for swimmers and ease of view to all guests: it could not have been better.

We were near the end of the allowed time with the whale sharks so I called the boat driver and asked him to put his earpiece in so we could speak in private. I outlined my idea to play Santa. The boat driver did not share François' and my naval background and was quite perplexed, but I said not to worry about the details and just direct the children to look towards the helicopter, and then try not to run me over when I was in the water.

We were ahead of the tender and a few hundred metres short of the yacht when François pulled the helicopter into a hover and we agreed this was a good spot; by eye, it may have been 15–20 metres above the water. I put my Santa hat on, put my waterproof satchel inside a small red bag that came with the costume and unclipped my five-point harness. Before opening the door, I used my last moment with the headset to confirm all was OK for the pilot. His smile was enough, and he said it was fine for him for me to keep going. I took the headset off, opened the door and stepped out to the landing skids. In any skydiving or helicopter jump, it was always the noise when the door was opened that confronted me and increased my heart rate; the jump itself was secondary.

The children were bouncing around on the front of the boat; the bow door had been raised again and they were leaning against it, waving frantically. I kept one hand to my Santa hat and tried my best to use the other to wave to the children while leaning, half in, half out of the helicopter cabin. Once I thought the theatre had been sufficiently staged, I jumped. Eyes to the horizon, feet together and one last wave before bringing my arms in.

Hitting the water was all good: no pain from the shoulders and, just as importantly, none from between the legs. If you have ever jumped into the water from anything higher than the edge of the swimming pool, you can understand my concern: shoulders and soft flesh were not designed for high-speed water impact. As I put my arms out to pull to the surface, I realised I was still going down, and quickly. It was only a couple of seconds, but things were not going to the plan shaped in my mind. Who would have thought that a Santa suit would cling so heavily and make it so hard to pull to the surface? The question is rhetorical, as it is pretty evident in hindsight that a weighty suit designed for shopping malls would not make for great swimming. My legs could not kick, and my arms were making little ground in their pulls.

I have had many events in my life where possibly I was putting my life at risk, but the two that came closest to seeing me shuffle off this mortal coil have been the most embarrassing. The first was back in Australia when I was almost crushed by a large stunt kite. Now in my second close brush with eternity, I am looking at drowning dressed as Santa. I stopped kicking, gave way to the sensation of sinking and tried to shrug the jacket clear of my arms. As a lifelong surfer I can find some sense of calm being held under, but still it was difficult to get the flannel sleeves off my arms and my anxiety was building. It doesn't take long when you are moving away from the surface for it all to feel very wrong. In what felt like a marathon, but was closer to 15 seconds, my arms were clear and I pulled to the surface.

I surfaced, pulled a great gasp of air, and turned to see if I could spot one of our boats. I saw the helicopter in the distance making its final approach to the yacht and then saw in the foreground our boat approaching me slowly. The bow door was being lowered and the children were still waving. Somewhere, I had lost my satchel with the sweets, but in the stillness of the Maldivian waters it was resting on the surface not more than 2 metres from me. I had the Santa hat in my hand, no idea how, and with my treats in the satchel I was back in business.

I rolled onto the boat and distributed the treats as a semi-Santa, the jacket still around my waist, held in place by the comically sized belt. There were cheers all round for a great event. I withdrew to the rear of the boat, leaving the guests to enjoy their time together. My gaze drifted to the horizon and I recalled something I had said to this yacht owner during first interviews: 'Never ask me to work harder. You get 100 per cent of what I have to offer. If it is not good enough, we can speak, and we can look for someone else because I will have no more to give.'

Every modern fitness guide will confirm that training is meant to be done in a cycle and 100 per cent commitment on every outing will only lead to fatigue and injury. The same is true in the workplace: commitment is important but against some popular teachings I have to remind myself constantly to hold back my 100 per cent. I find it a challenging balance to work hard but in a measured manner, to hold back and accept that there will be periods of reduced intensity/productivity that will help me build back to full strength. Showing ultimate commitment is a cliché for the junior employee during interview to confirm that they will give their undivided attention and all their passion, at all times: even if it is truthful, it is not realistic.

I still have trouble remembering to hold something back, to remember it is not always wise to jump with the Santa suit. I am blessed or cursed by a good deal of energy that needs to be managed for my sake and for those I work with. This is a work in progress, and I hope to get there some day.

Manage the peaks and troughs

Resist the corporate trope: 'I will give you 100 per cent.' This is not sustainable for you or your employer.

It is truly OK to communicate when you are below your sought-after or published performance level. It is most likely that before you say it, those around you have noticed anyway.

This candour can be reversed for leaders: when one of your team is having a flat period, speak to them: there might be a cause and there might not. In either case, raising it as a normal event takes the pressure out for both sides.

There is good reason why the Olympics are held four-yearly and not weekly. Peaks and troughs need to be managed.

The helicopter view

When talking with friends about the yacht owners I've worked with, once we've got through the 'how do they party' question, they will often ask for details of the 'secret sauce', the flash of brilliance that the billionaires must show. I have read my share of the big CEO 'hey look at me' books and listened to countless interviews. They are amazingly consistent: the authors and speakers present themselves as big-picture people maintaining a helicopter view – luckily without Santa suits. The interviews always get to a point where, through an overly white smile, the CEO will say: 'I just hire great people and then I stand back and let it all happen.' Yep, this is all bullshit… all the billionaire yacht owners of my lived experience are chronic micro-managers. They 'sweat the small shit' constantly: details matter to them, in their businesses and in their private lives.

It is not uncommon to sit with a billionaire for more than an hour, with several staff, obsessing over the place settings at the table. Who sits where, size of cards, font – and this is not for a wedding, but for Wednesday night. It matters. Sometimes it is financial, the billionaire making the point that they are not to be taken advantage of. More often, it is just in their nature and a key component of their incredible and hard-to-place success.

This is not my core nature and it is an attribute I am unable to emulate. I seek to empower and allow others to take control of the outcomes in their professional areas, to be the captains of their environment. Maybe I did listen to one too many of those scripted interviews about sitting back and taking the helicopter view and ignored the reality I was witnessing for 20 years. Maybe, more truthfully, I was not willing to compromise my nature to learn from this behaviour, regardless of its tenacity within the billionaire yacht owners I spent time with. I would rather, as my opening gambit, trust the information being given to me and by extension trust the person sharing it with me. This is not the case with the billionaire: they challenge and probe, never trusting the information until it has been deconstructed and evidenced.

Anchored in the Bay of Cannes, awaiting the madness of the film festival, the yacht owner made a cheeky entrance to the bridge. I say a cheeky entrance as there was a hidden, rarely used staircase from his day room on the deck below to the starboard side of the bridge. The yacht was preparing for a large function the next night and aside from attending to meals for the yacht owner and his wife, the crew and I were completing preparations with no great attention to their presence. He too was focused on ensuring the guest event was of the highest order and accepted the lack of attention to his personal needs in support of the higher cause.

The chief stewardess was also on the bridge at the time. She was showing me the etching of the yacht's logo on the champagne flutes we had commissioned at the yacht owner's request. We both paused to greet and acknowledge the presence of the yacht owner. He politely asked us both not to stop on his account but followed up by asking to see the embossed glasses. So we stopped and attended to his request. 'This is lovely. How many were made?' The chief stewardess agreed with the yacht owner's compliment on the quality and said we had 400 flutes embossed with what was quite an intricate logo. He nodded and asked, 'Why so many?' The chief stewardess remained on firm ground. 'The cost per unit was greatly reduced when we ordered above 300 and it was well worth it to have at least a hundred more than we expect to use for breakages into the future.'

The yacht owner nodded, turned the flute in his hand and passed it back to the chief stewardess. 'Captain, did you negotiate the cost?' There was a mild but discernible shift in his tone, and I was aware that this was not a question to be glibly dismissed. 'Yes, of course, I negotiated the firm down from a minimum of 500 units and in doing so reduced the cost by 20 per cent.' This was correct, but I did not elaborate that the firm was a family business who, to make the deadline, had brought their teenage children in over a weekend to deliver at such short notice. They were a delight to work with and took such pride in their work that I was embarrassed to be pushing a hard-negotiating position on behalf of a billionaire owner of a low-cost airline. While I was processing these thoughts, I could see the yacht owner's nods were slow and deliberate: we were not finished.

'What was the cost per unit?' At this point I drew breath, and although it was very slight, I think in review my sigh might have just snuck into the 'visible body language' spectrum. In a flat tone, I said, 'Two euros and 20 cents per glass.' I then received a tearing apart for my lack of concern for his wealth and while I knew to my core that this was far from the case, I obediently took the verbal beating.

I was embarrassed for the chief stewardess, who was witness to the full exchange. She was now in my peripheral vision, but I could see she was studying her shoes with unnecessary intensity. The yacht owner finished, turned and took the four paces to depart the bridge, again via his private staircase. As his hand touched the banister, he turned to face me once more. 'I am sorry for my behaviour and I know you work hard for me, but if I did not watch everything so closely, I would not have this yacht and you would not have employment.' He then turned and departed. I was impressed by his admission and his self-awareness, but I was equally aware that, regardless of the rewards, I would never emulate this behaviour. If this prohibited me from achieving the heights attained by my yacht owner, then that would be the cost.

Was this yacht owner merely putting on a show of his obsession to detail to keep me in check? Was he actually the 'strategy' and the 'big picture' guy? Naaah, he and his billionaire peers are micro-managers to their inner core. I have learned an incredible amount from my exposure to the world's billionaires. I am an unashamed watcher and

233

they have given me much to watch. Their behaviours have shown an insight into what it takes to create, develop and then live with incredible financial success. I have taken some of these behaviours into my own life and benefited from them – I do value time and I do try to give my full attention in conversation – but equally I have discarded other observed actions where the reward is less than the personal cost. The obsession to detail that my billionaires display can be admired from a distance in the way I may admire the evolutionary efficiency of a great white shark, while knowing it is something I do not seek to bring into my own life.

When perfect is not good enough

While writing this book I was interviewed for a podcast, and one of the questions from the interviewer was, 'As a superyacht captain, how do you manage the expectations of the yacht owner and their guests?'

A simple question, but when it is unpacked it becomes rather more complex. Let's think of a sample 100-metre yacht. The cost may exceed €200 million and the yacht owner has probably waited five years for it: two years of development with designers and brokers, and three years in construction. When their dream is finally delivered, how does a superyacht captain manage this expectation? You cannot. There is no way to perfectly match the near infinite expectations an owner has built up over the years as he waits patiently for delivery day.

To take it further, how should the captain deliver bad news to this new yacht owner? News that may reflect that the yacht does not function in the manner presented during the design, sales and construction cycle? The ribbon-cutting photo may be sitting in a frame and the sales brochure open on the web browser, but the actors belong to a time long forgotten: all shortcomings are directed to the captain. The honeymoon is over and there is a risk of a breakdown in the owner/captain relationship.

I had left Sardinia, Italy, and was soon to arrive in Nice, France, in a 100-metre yacht. It was early summer, and everything was going well. The yacht was ready, the crew were ready and the yacht owner, with family and their guests, were in the air on their way to join from the United States. This is a scene that occurs many times every day in the Mediterranean summer, with yachts meeting their guests adjacent to Nice airport at the small port of Saint-Laurent-du-Var.

The yacht was proceeding at a comfortable speed, and I was on the bridge more to keep the officer of the watch company than to maintain the navigation. The phone next to my chair rang, and the chief engineer spoke rapidly over the noise of the engines: 'The starboard propulsion motor… something is wrong, stop the ship!'

For the engineer to call and issue such a directive might be a once in a career event for him and I took it seriously. It was navigationally safe so I stopped the ship, instructed the officer of the watch to be very attentive to other shipping and call me if I was needed, and then went down the six decks to the control room to learn more. As I entered the room, to my surprise the full mechanical and electrical engineering teams were there. I expected the majority of the engineers to be addressing the problem, whatever it was. In a sombre, funereal tone, the chief engineer explained that the cooling water system for the propulsion motor had first sprung a leak and then completely disintegrated, destroying all electronics in its path. With the yacht owner on his way, there was no time to deconstruct how we came to be where we were: I needed to have enough facts to detail the situation and a firm timeline for repairs. The chief engineer said the frequency converter needed for propulsion was not useable and without contact with the manufacturer his first estimate would be a month, if not longer.

The return walk to the bridge felt eternal as I began to think through my next communications. I did not have enough firm facts. I could neither pad the story with a 'worst case' nor blithely talk down the repair. I also did not have the time to gather inputs from more sources; it was the weekend (it always is) and the plane was in the air. I had to get a short message to the owner, and fast. I churned over five lines of an electronic message for 15 minutes, adding words, changing phrasing and reordering the sentences. When I thought I was ready, I asked the chief engineer to join me to make sure my representation of the facts was 100 per cent. The message had to be mine alone and I was not looking for my colleague to shoulder the responsibility, but I had no room to misrepresent the situation. The chief engineer agreed to the content as being a truthful representation.

Dear XXXXX,

Earlier this morning the vessel suffered a catastrophic failure to one of the frequency converters, reducing the yacht to operating on a single propeller. In this configuration the maximum speed is seven knots and dynamic positioning is not possible. The yacht remains capable of receiving guests, but operating capabilities are severely limited. Exact repair time is not known, it requires the manufacture of new components and first indications are that it will be more than four weeks. All crew are crestfallen by this system failure. I am available immediately to speak with you on this.

My focus was to use the fewest words to convey the impact to the yacht owner and not take up the space with the details of the failure. Past learning had taught me to make sure the impact to the owner's experience was the focus and not the details of the incident (the yacht being only a platform to host their experience). Past experience is a great guide but cannot be relied upon, so a longer message was sent in parallel to the executive assistant accompanying the flight; this message had the technical details I had validated with the chief engineer.

The executive assistant is an essential link to the owner and I was fortunate that we had a good one. His first response to my message – 'Oh fuck!' – was as neat as anything I could have expected. I knew he would take the time to sit with the owner and brief him using the details we had provided. My assumption was confirmed as in rapid fire I started to receive messages seeking amplification: 'What is a frequency converter?' 'Why is one failure stopping us?' 'Is there not a spare?' These are the grasping questions that come fast and need to be answered at the same speed.

Over the next hour I wrote constantly across multiple messaging platforms and took around 12 calls of not more than 30 seconds, each call being another path being explored.

I was 99 per cent focused on the guest impact with only 1 per cent left for the actual priority: the critical failure of a primary system. I had delegated this to the chief officer and chief engineer with clear direction: keep the yacht safe, develop options for a safe haven and only interrupt me if anything escalates. The two had their mission objectives and moved independently. As my engagement with the owner, his personal assistants, the guests' personal assistants, the aviation staff and security began to taper, I asked for the chief officer's brief on options. He proposed the yacht enter Nice port.

The Port of Nice and its pilots are exceptional, and interactions are always a professional pleasure. The port had acknowledged the reduced manoeuvrability of the vessel and offered a berth for the yacht in a location I knew, Quai Riboty. On first pass it sounded fair, though at over 100 metres I did not expect the yacht would fit. I said the same to the chief officer, who shared that the port could not guarantee the tenure at the normal docks for a yacht of this size due to commercial traffic. In further support, the port pilot, whom we knew well, had said to the chief officer that we would squeeze in and that he knew he and I were capable together.

I trusted the Nice pilot and I trusted the chief officer. I had little option. I asked for a plan to be developed in accordance with this advice and that I be briefed not later than 30 minutes before planned entry, and at this point I would stop external communications and focus my attention on visualising the manoeuvre. I already had a navigation chart showing on the spare computer screen to help me begin building the mental model that I do for all manoeuvres. This may have been due to the mariner's prudence I have already described as developing through my career, or maybe I wanted to have something aside from the owner's combination of wrath and disappointment to focus on.

I had one hour to develop an outcome for the owners and their guests. I am good in these situations and am often guided by an interview that I saw with Grant Dalton, CEO of the America's Cup Team New Zealand. The interviewer had asked of Dalton what had been the change after his team's terrible defeat at the hands of Oracle Team USA in San Francisco in 2013. The loss caused deep soul-searching from Team New Zealand as they considered another challenge. It was in one of these sessions that Grant Dalton said, 'Throw the ball out as far as you can, nothing is off limits.' The strategy worked. Team New Zealand, with sailors riding bikes on board and a raft of innovations, regained the Cup, the Holy Grail of yacht racing, and this concept was forever etched in my consciousness. Embracing the spirit of Dalton and 'throwing the ball', I worked with others to deliver a creative solution involving another yacht for the guests to use.

With 40 minutes to the port, I began my preparation for the compromised entry. The weather was good, the team were behind me and the pilot would be a great asset when he boarded. I enjoyed the next 20 minutes finding my docking focus: we slowed to almost a halt adjacent to the imposing Cap de Nice to allow the pilot to board and for he and I to discuss our plan. As I waited for the pilot to make his way to the bridge, I scanned the headland of Mont Boron to the east of the port and lost myself in thought. Yvonne and I had lived in this area 15 years earlier – such great memories for us in a time when we were still defining how our journey together might be. I don't think I would have foreseen our life as we are living it, but I wouldn't have changed anything in the times we had spent together.

I was taken from my reminiscences by the warm greeting from the tall pilot as he entered the bridge. Working his hands together he said to the bridge team in his heavy Marseille-accented English, 'We are going to have some fun today!' He and I then spent five minutes going through every point of the port entry. We spoke about speeds, headings to look for and then the all-important final resting place. Once we had done this together, we repeated the conversation for the bridge team and officers in charge of the crew handling our berthing lines. As is so often the case, the pilot's and my confidence overshadowed the concerns of the officers and deck team. I was relaxed but missing the presence of the chief officer, who had been seconded to arrange the transfer of equipment for the guests to the replacement yacht and would remain there for two days to assist. This was the correct priority, but I missed him being there. We had become a strong team and I trusted his counsel.

We had overcome any nervousness he may have had at expressing his opinion if he did not agree with something, especially if it was with regards safety. At the end of the briefing, I tried to think, in his absence, what would have been his challenge to pierce my bubble of confidence in this manoeuvre. I could not think of anything specific, but my memory recalled the long-ago steering failure in the Loire River and I asked the pilot if the port's workboat could be available if needed to be a standby tug. The pilot agreed this was a good idea and arranged it via radio.

We began our approach. The port turned the entry lights to red to ensure we would be the only vessel moving in and out. We were very slow as we turned to the west for the entry, and I hoped we were not inconveniencing too many other yachts on a busy weekend. My time to reflect and reminisce had passed and I maintained my focus (though as we passed abeam 'Le Plongeoir' restaurant, I allowed myself the indulgence of remembering a magnificent birthday lunch Yvonne and I had shared there). Entering into the port, Le Plongeoir passed from sight and at 2 knots we were committed to the single-engine entry. Ship handling in such perfect conditions is somewhere between a meditation and a trance for me. My mind is clear of all the normal background noises and wonderfully occupied by the action and response of engines, rudders and the resultant vessel movement. When it all works, time passes lightly and the reward is the perfect motion of the vessel on its intended track with only minimal power.

The yacht was gliding, I was in my flow, and with the relaxed narrative of the pilot by my side I realised we had made the 160-degree turn to the north to align with Quai Riboty. The yacht was moving at a very slow walking pace, parallel and 5 metres displaced from the dock wall. The pilot had the port workers calling the distance ahead and astern – we all knew there was less than a metre of clearance, and we were reliant on the port workers. I would hear their report in French to the pilot and internalise the distance before the pilot repeated it to me in English out of professional courtesy. 'Six mètres de plus' – I looked to the dock 12 metres below my feet to gauge what this might feel like; looking ahead did not help, as due to the height of the bow the first thing I could see was a building 60 metres ahead.

The propulsion of the yacht was two propellers that rotated 360 degrees on an 'azipull' motor. These, in combination with a tunnel thruster forward, made for an incredibly responsible platform, and once mastered this installation is the nirvana of manoeuvrability. It is not the standard configuration and not all captains have experience with such a system. On this day, with only one azipull functioning, I had to anticipate well ahead to allow the motor to rotate.

In the chief officer's absence, I had one of the more junior officers by my side radioing to the deck to adjust their lines. I had spoken to him earlier of the importance of precise, yet relaxed guidance to the deck crew working the lines.

He was doing well, and I could hear him saying, 'Ease the forespring, 3 metres, just steady.' The forespring was the line coming from the very front of the yacht and leading back 70 metres on the dock, where it was looped onto the cast-iron bollard. It was our brake and the most important tool available to us to stop the yacht continuing forward and impacting with the dock ahead.

Maintaining his relaxed tone, the pilot asked me to come a little closer to the dock as we drew closer to our final position. I looked up and saw that the mast of a sailboat seemed improbably close to our bow: we were only 1 metre from the other boat. I used the bow thruster to bring the yacht 2 metres closer to the wall and increase the distance to the sailboat, 'quatre mètres de plus'. Really? How could I come ahead four more metres when it already looked like the front of the yacht was extending over the service road of the port and the small sailboat looked like it was soon to be fully underneath our bow. Instinctively, before the pilot repeated in English, I had drawn the yacht to a virtual halt. The slow walking pace had become an imperceptible crawl. Little escapes a seasoned pilot, and he said, 'It's OK, Captain, keep coming, we are watching everything for you and it is safe.' My reply was a small movement ahead on the propulsion lever: I was in my flow and did not need to speak.

For the last time I heard the deck officer instruct the foredeck to ease two more metres and I broke from my deep concentration only when I heard a change in tone from the dock radio: 'En position, bravo.' With 75 centimetres clearance ahead, we were precisely where Port of Nice had said we would finish. The pilot knew he was good and before I thanked him, I let him bask in his success for a moment as he radioed the port to confirm his plan had been successful.

One hour later, the bridge was empty. I was alone, completely drained from all the adrenaline that had been flowing since the first call from the chief engineer. I knew that docking the yacht was inconsequential compared to the fallout from the weight of the disappointment I had conveyed to the owner. I loved my job as a captain, but I envied the carefree crew beginning to go ashore to take advantage of an unexpected opportunity to walk the streets of Nice port. In contrast, I had a knot in my stomach that would not shift, and a sense of lethargy that seemed to pin me to the bridge chair for the longest time.

I looked back to Mont Boron, now very close to the east of the yacht, and tried to identify 'La Petite Maison', the little house Yvonne and I had shared in more carefree times. The golden light of early evening flowed into the bridge windows and the port was at its most beautiful, but nothing was lifting the weight. I should have been walking with the crew and reflecting on a successful day. The yacht was safe, the engineering rectification works had already begun and the chief engineer had tracked down a reliable representative from the manufacturer who would travel on Sunday night to arrive the next morning. All this did not change the fact that, through no specific fault of mine, the yacht was effectively removed from service to its owner and guests. Yes, the guests were on an alternative yacht and this should have felt like a success. But it wasn't – I knew it and, more importantly, so did the owner.

Over the subsequent weeks I dwelt on the events of that first day, as the full extent of the system damage became apparent. I developed a document, a detailed report that recorded the time, information available and factors supporting my decisions from the beginning and extending into the subsequent weeks. I highlighted the inflection points where decisions needed to be made and accompanied each with a flow chart that supported my choices. It was a good report and I pored over it late into some nights: it was my catharsis.

I shared the document regularly with my upstream managers, changing the edition as each update extended the decision path. As I had lived through so often in my career, I discovered that the more consequential the decision, the less middle management stepped up to be counted. Ordering T-shirts or toothpaste would elicit impassioned views on costs and quality, whereas this event, which would ultimately cost close to €1 million, received no external actionable comment. All heads were being kept well below the parapet.

Regardless of the willingness or not of others to carry some weight, writing a record helped me reflect and deconstruct in slow time whether I had made the correct decisions. With the clarity of time, I had, and there was nothing more I could have done. My leadership strategies throughout were sound, drawing on all the expertise available and pushing for multiple solution paths, 'throwing the ball as far as I could' and even assisting the guests to be settled on another yacht for their holiday. All communications were concise and timely and my challenging all parties consulting on the repairs ensured the swiftest reparations. Collectively, this came to nil as the yacht wallowed in the Port of Nice.

Most of my greatest learning outcomes are from my admission of a personal shortcoming or failing. The mechanical failure on approach to the Port of Nice is an outlier – I really did do everything correctly. I can say this with the confidence of having deconstructed almost every action too many times to recall. Regardless, it caused an irreparable tear in my relationship with the yacht owner that nothing, not even time, could overcome.

A lesson worth learning

With this I learned my greatest lesson: I could never allow someone else's judgement of my actions to define me.

Too many times I have received praise, when I snuck through with some luck on my side: on these occasions I accepted the praise but was brutal with my self-critique.

In this case, I accepted all the admonitions of failure but knew this had been one of my greatest successes.

TIME TO SAY GOODBYE

The realisation that my best, a best that over 20 years had become as good as any superyacht captain, was to be judged as a failure left me to question the full validity of all I had strived to deliver. I knew the problem was not mine, but it remained a question that maybe it was time to allow those I had led to take their place as leaders. I stepped ashore in early 2020, before the enormity of the year had begun to unfold. I was asked many times if I had given up seafaring for good. The honest response is that I don't know. When I look to the mountains of Austria or tend my ever-expanding garden, a part of me is yearning for the Southern Ocean swells on a calm day, or the rush of trying to outmanoeuvre three hurricanes in the Atlantic. I think that after a time to regather, I will return to the environment I know so well, but it will be a more reflective version of my former self. I will react with less pace but hopefully more precision. I will listen more attentively and verbalise my praise for others, and likewise say out loud my concerns for my own performance.

When I at last passed my final captain's exams, some 13 years after starting the journey, I was so surprised and in awe of achieving something I had viewed in the abstract that I dissociated my shy self from the captaincy to the point where I looked to the role I held as though it were not me at all but a third party. This is hard to fully communicate, but it was true of this time – since I was so proud that part of me had achieved captaincy, I expected everyone else to view this part of me with the same awe. They didn't, of course, and my pride was mistaken for arrogance. I can see this now and would like to circle back to the people at the time and correct this, but perceptions are owned by those perceiving and to seek to change them would only bring a fresh round forward.

I never allowed the yacht or my role within it to define me. I was always aware that when not sailing as captain I remained largely a shy, introspective person, identifying more with the slightly overweight 11-year-old who found himself locked in a hotel walk-in freezer while trying to snack on chocolate than some gilded vision of the billionaire's captain. Nevertheless, I had walked the captain's path and grown through the incredible experiences afforded to seafarers. The word 'journey' is one that I am often mocked for using, but I do not shy away from it. Life, leadership, learning and loving are all journeys and I hope through sharing some of my experiences that it may be interesting, insightful and even helpful. I wonder how the book may have read if I had been morally courageous and completed my studies towards a career in indigenous education? Likely, it may have been even better.

As someone who has always been most proud of my shortcomings, this extract from a speech made by Theodore Roosevelt resonates:

> *It is not the critic who counts; not the man who points out how the strong man stumbles, or where the doer of deeds could have done them better. The credit belongs to the man who is actually in the arena, whose face is marred by dust and sweat and blood; who strives valiantly; who errs, and comes short again and again, because there is no effort without error and shortcoming; but who does actually strive to do the deeds; who knows the great enthusiasms, the great devotions; who spends himself in a worthy cause; who at the best knows in the end the triumph of high achievement, and who at the worst, if he fails, at least fails while daring greatly, so that his place shall never be with those cold and timid souls who know neither victory nor defeat.*
>
> *Roosevelt: Citizenship in a Republic, 23 Apr 1910*

I am proud of my career and while I know Roosevelt may never have thought of his citizen as a superyacht captain, with some sweat but no dust and blood, I draw strength from his words. I have, since my youth, always stepped forward, more often than not tripping as I did so. I think the only great regret one can have in life is not to try.

I have dared, I have failed, and I have done it many times.

ENDNOTE

Throughout every story, I have sought to be truthful to my memory and represent my emotions at the time. Given that the arc exceeds 35 years, I am aware that my recall has been sliced by the ravages of time: sometimes a story is retold so often it becomes the driver, and I the passenger, to the tale. I hope this is not the case on too many occasions, but I accept that my memory of a day 20 years past may vary to that of the person I was sitting next to at the time.

Returning to the introduction, this was never to be a 'kiss and tell' of the yachting community and those who play their roles within it. Yes, an informed reader may recognise details in a tale and may even be able to identify what and who is involved. To avoid this entirely would dilute to where the taste would be lost. Where I think there might be any negativity, I have sought to place enough of a veil to obscure the bride. Some names are changed, some are not, and others are just not mentioned. And what about my captain in Mykonos? He remained working for the same family for many years and had an exceptional career, we all have off days.

As much as I enjoy writing, I love reading more. I do not hide that many insights are my repackaging of the thinking of those who have walked ahead of me. I chanced upon a wonderful quote from Shane Parrish of Farnam Street: '[helping you] master the best of what other people have already figured out.' I don't claim any greater insight than what my experiences and my reading have given me.

Fair winds and following seas, my friends.

Your most humble and obedient servant,

Brendan